New Directions for
Higher Education

Martin Kramer
EDITOR-IN-CHIEF

D1538491

Restructuring
Shared Governance
in Higher
Education

William G. Tierney
Vicente M. Lechuga
EDITORS

Number 127 • Fall 2004
Jossey-Bass
San Francisco

RESTRUCTURING SHARED GOVERNANCE IN HIGHER EDUCATION
William G. Tierney, Vicente M. Lechuga (eds.)
New Directions for Higher Education, no. 127
Martin Kramer, Editor-in-Chief

Microfilm copies of issues and articles are available in 16mm and 35mm, as well as microfiche in 105mm, through University Microfilms Inc., 300 North Zeeb Road, Ann Arbor, Michigan 48106-1346.

NEW DIRECTIONS FOR HIGHER EDUCATION (ISSN 0271-0560, electronic ISSN 1536-0741) is part of The Jossey-Bass Higher and Adult Education Series and is published quarterly by Wiley Subscription Services, Inc., a Wiley Company, at Jossey-Bass, 989 Market Street, San Francisco, California 94103-1741. Periodicals Postage Paid at San Francisco, California, and at additional mailing offices. POSTMASTER: Send address changes to New Directions for Higher Education, Jossey-Bass, 989 Market Street, San Francisco, California 94103-1741.

New Directions for Higher Education is indexed in Current Index to Journals in Education (ERIC); Higher Education Abstracts.

SUBSCRIPTIONS cost $80 for individuals and $170 for institutions, agencies, and libraries. See ordering information page at end of book.

EDITORIAL CORRESPONDENCE should be sent to the Editor-in-Chief, Martin Kramer, 2807 Shasta Road, Berkeley, California 94708-2011.

Cover photograph © Digital Vision

www.josseybass.com

CONTENTS

EDITORS' NOTES

Shared governance has been a hallmark of higher education in the United States since the early twentieth century. Since the inception of the idea, faculty, administrators, trustees, and other interested parties have either bemoaned or celebrated it. In 1915, Dewey, who helped start the American Association of University Professors (AAUP), spoke of the importance of faculty involvement in the decisions of the institution. In 1918, Veblen wrote a stinging attack on academic life in *The Higher Learning in America* and lamented the control that business interests had over academics irrespective of shared governance. Some critics have written of the lethargic pace of decision making brought on by the involvement of academics (Association of Governing Boards of Universities and Colleges, 2001), and still others have noted that shared governance may have worked well at some point, but so did dinosaurs (Kellogg Commission on the Future of State and Land-Grant Colleges, 1996).

Our purpose here is neither to side with those who celebrate shared governance nor with those who seek its demise. Rather, we offer a variety of viewpoints that will bring to light various ways one may think of shared governance. The intent is to foment dialogue and debate about the shape of shared governance for the future. Our assumption is that many challenges are at academe's doorstep that may require significant changes. If those of us who work in colleges and universities are not well organized to deal with those challenges, then the solutions that we develop will be love's labors lost. Governance is the means to implementing ideas that either respond to problems or provide new strategies. If academic governance is ineffective, then it needs to be reformed. The shape of those reforms is what the authors of this volume consider.

Robert Birnbaum begins the volume, in Chapter One, by arguing for the premise that guided the idea of shared governance throughout the twentieth century. Shared governance, suggests Birnbaum, is not merely a decision-making structure that is either good or bad, effective or ineffective. Shared governance is also a symbol and ideology of academic life. The author strenuously takes issue with what he sees as a management fad for greater administrative prerogative. By way of careful analyses of the organizational literature, Birnbaum suggests that the diminution of the faculty role in governance is likely to have a reverse effect—institutional effectiveness will be decreased, not increased.

In Chapter Two, Gabriel Kaplan begins with an entirely different premise. He wonders if governance even matters. He rightly points out that critics and supporters of shared governance begin from the same starting point: governance makes a difference. By way of a national survey of those engaged in shared governance, Kaplan tests the validity of such an assumption. He concludes that governance actually may not make a direct difference on outcomes; there are, however, indirect effects. He cautions researchers, administrators, and policymakers alike not to overemphasize the import of one or another structure. He suggests, for example, that a resource-dependency approach would place much more emphasis on the external environment than on internal structural issues and that such a focus may be more fruitful.

In Chapter Three, Adrianna Kezar agrees with Kaplan in some respects. However, Kezar emphasizes not external variables but internal relationships. Her assumption is that the culture of the organization plays a larger role in enabling organizational effectiveness than does governance. By way of an interpretive perspective, Kezar argues that an organization's structures and governance processes are more symbolic than real. Accordingly, rather than focus on how to improve governance by changing shared governance, she suggests that one needs to develop understandings of what ideas such as "trust" imply for academic life.

Paul Lingenfelter disagrees in Chapter Four. Governance does matter, he suggests, and current arrangements are insufficient. He offers the perspective of state officials who have become increasingly disenchanted with not simply the way colleges and universities govern themselves, but more important, what they do. He does not call for state intervention into academic life, but he points out that the evolving purposes of higher education necessitate structural changes. He offers a caution and warning: If postsecondary institutions do not reform themselves, then they will be reformed. States have become increasingly aggressive about how they organize governing boards; the author does not see states becoming any less relentless in pursuit of accountability, which will necessitate different ways of governing.

In Chapter Five, William Mallon returns the focus to the internal organization of governance, but he provides a twenty-first century twist. Throughout the twentieth century, the academic department was the building block of academic life. Shared governance occurred not only in institutional structures such as academic senates but also—some would say primarily—in schools and departments where much of the work of academic life got done. Mallon points out that the internal organization of many of the nation's premier research universities has undergone structural change without anyone noticing. He employs the useful metaphor of the suburbs, suggesting that the rapid rise of research centers and institutes (the suburbs) have significant implications for how the core academic institution (the cities) govern themselves. Just as in real life, urban flight not only creates changes in the areas that are being built up, it also suggests that the cities have dramatically different arrangements. In this case, no one is quite sure what will eventually happen, but the implications for governance are significant if academic departments are no longer the building blocks of academic life.

Myron Pope opens up an entirely new way of thinking about governance in Chapter Six by calling on the literature on trust. The idea of trust, as Kezar mentions, has been underutilized in the analysis of academic organizations; Pope points out, however, that it has become a topic of serious study and analysis in traditional organizations. Pope argues that trust needs to become as serious a topic of inquiry in research pertaining to colleges and universities. This chapter is less definitive and more exploratory insofar as so little research has been done in the area. What the author raises are a series of conceptual issues that need to be considered as a potentially useful new conceptual area is investigated.

Finally, in Chapter Seven, Tierney and Minor look less at whether governance matters or what vantage point should be employed to study it and instead consider the role of communication in governance. They agree both with Lingenfelter's assertion that some governance structures need to change and with Kaplan's argument that governance is not always the key to effectiveness; however, they suggest that one has to focus on communicative processes in all situations. They agree with Kezar about the importance of understanding the symbolic aspects of organizational life. In doing so, they suggest, communication becomes central to organizational effectiveness. They base their argument on a survey to several hundred institutions and case studies of a small subset.

Clearly, these chapters at times overlap and conflict with one another. Lingenfelter and Birnbaum, for example, most likely disagree with one another's premises. Kaplan even questions if governance matters, whereas the other authors all begin by assuming that governance can make a difference. Kezar, Pope, Tierney, and Minor work from an interpretive perspective, but all employ different strategies of interpretation; Mallon looks at structural transformations within the internal environment, and Lingenfelter considers the changes at work external to the organization.

Thus, this volume offers competing conceptions of what has been a key concept in academic life—shared governance. Our intent has not been to offer one doctrinaire approach to academic governance; no one direction is particularly clear or correct. Instead, we intend by way of these essays to stimulate thought and conversation about a key academic topic and how it might change in the coming years.

References

Association of Governing Boards of Universities and Colleges (AGB). *AGB Statement on Institutional Governance and Governing in the Public Trust; External Influences on Colleges and Universities.* Washington, D.C.: Association of Governing Boards of Universities and Colleges, 2001.

Dewey, J. "Introductory Address to the American Association of University Professors (January 1915)." In J. A. Boydston (ed.), *John Dewey: The Middle Works, 1899–1924,* Vol. 8: *1915.* Carbondale: Southern Illinois University Press, 1980.

Kellogg Commission on the Future of State and Land-Grant Colleges. *Taking Charge of Change: Renewing the Promise of State and Land-Grant Universities.* Washington, D.C.: National Association of State Universities and Land Grant Colleges, 1996.

Veblen, T. *The Higher Learning in America.* New York: Hill and Wang, 1957. (Originally published 1918.)

WILLIAM G. TIERNEY is the Wilbur-Kieffer Professor of Higher Education and director of the Center for Higher Education Policy Analysis, University of Southern California.

VICENTE M. LECHUGA is a research assistant in the Center for Higher Education Policy Analysis, University of Southern California, and is currently involved in a three-year research project that is analyzing and recommending ways to improve shared governance in four-year colleges and universities.

1

Proposals to make governance "more efficient" by reducing or limiting the faculty role in shared governance are likely to diminish institutional effectiveness.

The End of Shared Governance: Looking Ahead or Looking Back

Robert Birnbaum

Governance is the term we give to the structures and processes that academic institutions invent to achieve an effective balance between the claims of two different, but equally valid, systems for organizational control and influence. One system, based on legal authority, is the basis for the role of trustees and administration; the other system, based on professional authority, justifies the role of the faculty. The importance of legal authority was recognized with the founding of our first colleges. The acceptance of the role of professional authority is a more recent phenomenon that has evolved over time.

The original argument for faculty participation emphasized only their competence to deal with strictly academic matters. President Tappan of the University of Michigan, for example, proposed in 1858 that the faculty should enjoy sovereignty over teaching methods and the curriculum, since scholars "are the only workmen who can build up universities" (Tappan, 1961, p. 519). This principle, while broadly recognized, was honored more in the breach than in the observance by many institutions for the next fifty years. But the increasing professionalism of the faculty during the early decades of the twentieth century, accelerated by the academic revolution following World War II, led many institutions to accept not only faculty control over the curriculum but also a strong faculty voice in other education-related matters.

In 1967 the canonical "Statement on Government of Colleges and Universities" (American Association of University Professors, 2001), jointly formulated by three national associations and therefore often referred to as the Joint Statement, formally articulated and legitimated the faculty role in academic governance for the first time. Describing the essential relationship among trustees, presidents, and faculty as based on "mutual understanding," "joint effort," and "inescapable interdependence," the Joint Statement laid out two basic principles of what has come to be known as shared governance: first, important areas of action involve at one time or another the initiating capacity and decision-making participation of all the institutional components, and second, difference in the weight of each voice, from one point to the next, should be determined by the reference to the responsibility of each component for the particular matter at hand (American Association of University Professors, 2001, p. 218).

Not only did the Joint Statement confirm the faculty's "primary responsibility" for educational matters such as faculty status and programs of instruction and research, but it also articulated the importance of faculty involvement in educational policy more generally, including setting institutional objectives, planning, budgeting, and selecting administrators.

The various systems for consultation and decision making created by individual institutions to operationalize the shared aspects of governance appear today to be working well and are generally supported by both faculty and administrators (Cox, 2000). For example, senate chairs, academic vice presidents, and institutional presidents agree that campus senates operate efficiently and smoothly, consider important issues, and are believed to be associated with good communications and trust between institutional constituencies (Gilmour, 1991; Minor, 2003). Minor's study of four-year colleges and universities (2003) indicates that "shared governance remains a strong institutional value among all campus constituents" (p. 970). Nevertheless, there are increasing criticisms about the effectiveness of shared governance and proposals for radical change. These proposals do not challenge the role of trustees and administrators; their latent, if not manifest, purpose is to rationalize governance by reducing the involvement of the faculty in institutional decision making.

Current criticisms about academic governance focus attention on changes in the external environment and claim that, because of faculty obstructionism, contemporary governance systems cannot respond appropriately. In the words of the 1998 statement on governance by the Association of Governing Boards of Universities and Colleges (AGB), "Many governing boards, faculty members, and chief executives believe that internal governance arrangements have become so cumbersome that timely decisions are difficult to make, and small factions often are able to impede the decision-making process" (Association of Governing Boards of Universities and Colleges, 2001, p. 3). Among AGB's recommended solutions are that boards should reiterate their ultimate responsibility and authority, explicitly clarify who has the right to make or participate in specific kinds of decisions, establish deadlines to speed up decisions, and clarify ambiguous or overlapping areas of stakeholder authority.

There are dire warnings of the consequences if governance reforms are not enacted. "Institutions ignore a changing environment at their peril," said the National Association of State Universities and Land Grant Colleges. "Like dinosaurs, they risk becoming exhibits in a kind of cultural Jurassic Park: places of great interest and curiosity, increasingly irrelevant in a world that has passed them by" (Kellogg Commission on the Future of State and Land-Grant Colleges, 1996, p. 1). The dinosaur simile is evocative for anyone who has seen *Fantasia*, but perhaps should not be particularly distressing; after all, dinosaurs ruled the earth for more than 150 million years and might be the rulers still (thus making moot the problem of academic governance) but for an unpredictable and catastrophic asteroid impact.

Calls to revise governance systems to permit institutions to respond to the environment in a more timely fashion appear to accept two questionable assumptions: first, that today's colleges and universities have *not* been responsive enough, and second, that speed in making decisions is an asset in academic institutions.

The first assumption, that under existing governance arrangements institutions have not been responsive enough, is puzzling. Specific examples are seldom given and counterexamples are numerous. Institutions appear to be actively responding to environmental pressures by, for example, computerizing, raising external funds, establishing joint programs with industry, offering external degrees, and reducing full-time faculty. There are few, if any, emerging professions—and indeed few, if any, vocational or technical areas—that do not have academic programs dedicated to them. An alternative view, as Mingle (2000) has pointed out, is that "higher education, contrary to popular political belief, is in many ways extraordinarily responsive to the external environment—especially when that external environment demands market-driven solutions and orientations" (p. 10). As a consequence, "in striking new ways, American colleges and universities no longer look or act much as they did 30, or even 20, years ago" (Eckel, 2003, p. 865). The second assumption, concerning the speed of institutional decision making, is also problematic. The effectiveness of normative institutions is not based on efficiency and speed but on reliability and trust, and any process that makes it possible to make good decisions more quickly also makes it possible to make bad decisions more quickly. Faculty involvement in shared governance may slow down the decision-making process, but it also assures more thorough discussion and provides the institution with a sense of order and stability (Kerr, 1963). The greatest danger to higher education may not be that decisions are made too slowly because of the drag of consultation, but that they are made too swiftly and without regard for institutional core values. As Bok (2003) has commented, "The entrepreneurial university, it is said, must be able to move quickly. It cannot wait for windy faculty debates to run their course lest valuable opportunities be lost in the fast-moving corporate world in which we live. In fact, there is remarkably little evidence to support this view. Looking over the checkered history of commercial activity on campuses, one can much more easily point to examples of costly unilateral decisions by impatient administrators, such as ill-advised Internet ventures or grandiose athletic projects, than to valuable opportunities lost through inordinate faculty delays" (p. B9).

Bok's criticism suggests that the essential debate may not reflect differences about how a university should be *governed*, but rather conflicting ideologies and differences in belief about what a university should *be*. The complaints are not really about the inability to move quickly—they are about the inability to change a university quickly into something else. This chapter argues that governance and institutional purpose are related, and that proposals that suggest, either explicitly or implicitly, that the faculty role in shared governance should be reduced or limited are more likely to diminish rather than improve institutional effectiveness. It is important to differentiate first between two types of institutions, which I shall refer to as "academic" and "market," and next, between two separate aspects of governance, which I shall refer to as "hard" and "soft." It is also important to posit a relationship between institutional type and governance emphasis.

"Academic" and "Market" Institutions

Although the great diversity of colleges and universities is widely recognized, this appreciation has not been properly extended to an understanding of diversity in their governance. The culture, structure, programs, personnel, and technology of different institutions all influence participant expectations of how decisions are to be made and how influence is to be allocated. For that reason, conceptual discussions of the importance of "shared governance" are often fruitless unless the characteristics of the institutions being discussed are specified. To that end I will oversimplify a multidimensional construct by suggesting that institutions can be placed on a continuum of purpose anchored by polar types that I refer to as "academic" and "market." These types roughly correspond to the distinction that Gumport (2000b) has made between higher education as a social institution and as an industry; they also mirror the conflict described by Enders (2002) between "the university as the curiosity-driven institution in the cultural belief system, and as a service enterprise according to a utilitarian belief system" (p. 85).

Although all institutions of higher education have some admixture of academic and market elements, my comments about shared governance are meant to apply only to those institutions nearest the academic pole of the continuum; that is, those espousing norms and values that identify them as social institutions concerned with education primarily as an end and not as a means. Shared governance may often be frustrating and exasperating, but I believe that is the most effective process through which academic institutions can achieve their indefinite goals, just as concepts such as consent of the governed, checks and balances, and the right of legitimate yet contending voices to participate makes democracy itself ungainly yet ultimately effective. To the extent that institutions move away from the academic pole and emphasize education as a means rather than as an end by offering products based on consumer demand, deviations from shared governance may potentially be useful.

At the market extreme of the academic-market continuum, for example, there is no compelling reason for implementing processes and structures of shared governance. Consider a profit-making corporation such as the University of Phoenix, which markets vocationally oriented credentials and offers simplified and centrally planned, lowest-common-denominator curriculum materials capable of being "taught" in multiple locations by inexperienced, part-time employees. The "trustees" and "administration" are happy with their profits, the "faculty" are pleased with earning additional income without having to design their own classes, and the "students" are satisfied with earning degrees "quickly and with as little resistance as possible" (Farrell, 2003, p. A10). Faculty are transmitters of training material, not autonomous scholars; students are consumers purchasing products, not learners being educated. In such institutions, corporate structures and processes may not only be acceptable but in fact may improve both efficiency and effectiveness.

In contrast, academic institutions are those that give priority to education as an end in itself and are deeply rooted in a culture that prizes academic freedom, critical discourse, creativity, and liberal learning. Their normative institutional nature is illustrated by Kerr's reference to the university as "a church with a religion. It believes in the unfettered search for truth, in free expression of opinion without fear, in preservation of the past, including books, however offensive they may be currently, and in access on merit and the granting of grace on merit. Its principles are more important than service, or rules, or votes, or consumer preference. It is the keeper of the good, the true, and the beautiful; of culture. It perpetuates a spirit of inquiry and integrity. Its religion is not subject to compromise" (1970, p. 116). These are not market concepts but core values that are antithetical to the market (Ikenberry, 2001).

The academic versus market tension in higher education, in which academic institutions are compared to businesses, is not a new one. The arguments were the same about a hundred years ago when Andrew S. Draper, president of the University of Illinois, opined that "the university cannot become a business corporation, with a business corporation's ordinary implications. Such a corporation is without what is being called *spiritual aim,* is without moral methods. Universities are to unlock the truth and turn out the best and the greatest men and women. . . . A university cannot become such a [business] corporation without ceasing to be a university" (Draper, 1906, p. 36). Draper knew that proposals to change structure are at the same time proposals to change purpose and culture. And changing character and identity risks losing the core expertise, commitment to mission, and long-term perspective that gives the university its unique character (as well as what contemporary marketers would refer to as its "competitive advantage").

"Hard" and "Soft" Governance

"Hard" (or rational) governance refers to the structures, regulations, and systems of sanctions in an organization that define authority relationships, prescribe certain organizational processes and encourage compliance with enacted policies and procedures. "Soft" (or interactional) governance encompasses the systems of social connections and interactions in an organization that help to develop and maintain individual and group norms. Hard and soft governance are based on quite different conceptual foundations.

The theoretical underpinnings of hard governance are to be found in theories of rational choice. Rational actors are presumed to be "entirely forward looking, and entirely self-interested" (Blackburn, 1998, p. 29). Rational systems are based on calculations of costs and benefits, and are set in place to maximize the likelihood that certain desirable outcomes will occur in the future. Thus hard governance is forward-looking.

The theoretical foundations of soft governance are located in the concepts of how organizational cultures are created over time through the interaction of people and the cognitive processes through which people come collectively to share perceptions and "make sense" of what they are doing. Soft governance is backward-looking. The essence of soft governance is embedded in the socialization and expectations of the participants; institutions justify their behaviors, participants their roles, and society its support, based on their consistency with processes, roles, and missions established in the past.

Proposals to alter shared governance, such as those by AGB mentioned earlier, are predicated on a rationally based claim of cause and effect—that changing governance structure, and in particular those aspects of structure that affect the participation of faculty, will improve institutional performance. The history of attempts to reform hard governance does not provide a great deal of support for that claim. Nevertheless, there are continual calls for the reform of hard governance despite the lack of evidence that such changes would be consequential. This is due, in part, to the ideological belief that such changes should be consequential, and in part because such structural changes are, at least in theory, administratively feasible. Less attention is given to the normative issues of soft governance (Gumport, 2000a), in part because changes in hard governance often deny the importance of soft governance, and in part because no one knows how to go about altering soft governance.

While hard governance can channel and to some extent harness the power of soft governance so that the two are mutually reinforcing, in and of itself it appears to have little influence. As Kerr (1982) reported, "I once thought that alternative modes of governance had substantial significance in American higher education. . . . I would now advance the conclusion that, within the range of alternatives considered in the United States, forms of governance make some difference but not as much as often supposed. . . .

Given the heavy emphasis on individually made decisions by faculty members and the active competition among institutions, one specific arrangement in government versus another has minor implications for what actually happens in a university" (pp. 29–31).

Hard governance makes little difference because most of the important decisions made in the university occur outside the formal system. As Cohen and March (1974) have it, "Each individual in the university is seen as making autonomous decisions. Teachers decide if, and when, and what to teach. Students decide if, when, and what to learn. Legislators and donors decide if, when, and what to support. . . . The 'decisions' of the system are a consequence produced by the system but intended by no one and decisively controlled by no one" (p. 33).

Of course, it is precisely this lack of control that hard governance reformers seek to change, despite the generally accepted belief that the same lack of control has produced a system of higher education of unequaled quality and diversity. Ironically, it is usually those most philosophically supportive of a market economy who are among the first to suggest the need to rationalize systems when they don't care for what the market has produced.

Looking back on the failed governance innovations of the turbulent 1970s, Kerr (1982) remarked that "changes in formal governance have generally made little difference and, when they did, mostly for the worse. All that effort, all that passion, all that turmoil was mostly for naught. . . ." (p. 31). More recent attempts to change governance through the creation of such new structures as joint big decision committees (Yamada, 1991) seem to have met the same fate, as have numerous attempts over the last fifty years to impose on academic institutions rational management systems that, by altering decision-making processes, were also disguised attempts to change governance structures (Birnbaum, 2000). Hard governance proposals almost always sound reasonable and self-evident. But when they conflict with soft governance, they inevitably fail. Soft governance rules!

Isomorphism of Governance and Institutional Type

It was suggested earlier that shared governance may be important to the proper performance of an academic institution, but may be counterproductive in a market one. Governance may therefore be isomorphic with program. If so, attempts to change one will also change the other. If institutions become less academic, governance is less likely to be shared, and as governance is less shared, institutions are likely to become less academic. As the faculty role is diminished, declining trust in faculty leads to increasing interest in rational management (Gumport, 2000a); in the same way, implementing new management techniques may further reduce trust in faculty. The change from an academic to a market institution may be neither immediate nor direct—the loosely coupled properties of institutions will prevent that—but over time it is likely to occur; we have already seen that "academic planning, budgeting, and day-to-day administration are becoming more like the management processes developed for the private sector and increasingly reflect values that conflict with the traditional values of university governance" (Waugh, 2003, p. 85). Proposals to alter the management or governance systems of universities are really disguised (and sometimes not so disguised) attempts to make academic institutions into something else, so that the institutions lose "moral legitimacy, core purposes, and values such that [those institutions are] no longer recognizable and identified as the entity [they were] supposed to be (Gumport, 2000b, p. 85).

The Consequences of Proposed Governance Changes

All governance systems must deal with two issues: making good decisions, and getting those subject to such systems to accept the decisions as legitimate. People in general, and academics in particular, do not automatically accept the decisions of authorities. Boards of trustees, if they wished, could impose the governance recommendations of AGB on their institutions. Their legal right to do so is unquestioned and, although the Joint Statement recommends that boards undertake appropriate self-limitation, it recognizes them as the institution's final legal authority. Yet there are several reasons to believe that any unilateral actions to change the faculty role in shared governance would not be accepted, regardless of the promised effects on the institution or the exact nature of the new faculty role. Aside from issues of academic freedom that affected faculty would almost surely raise, such changes would violate principles of procedural justice, diminish faculty status, and reduce institutional social capital. As a consequence, levels of trust and cooperation would diminish, processes of social regulation would be compromised, and institutional viability as an academic (as opposed to a market) entity would be threatened.

Procedural Justice

Procedural justice refers to the perceived fairness of the processes through which organizational decisions are made. Fair processes may be desirable in all organizations, but they are of particular importance in normative organizations, such as colleges and universities, in which goals are unclear and the consequences of decisions are not easily assessed. Unable to obtain reliable feedback on decision outcomes, participants in what Deal and Kennedy (1982) term these "process cultures" instead focus their attention on how things are done (p. 108). Decisions made "in the right way" are more likely to be considered legitimate, and perceived legitimacy in turn makes voluntary compliance with social regulations more likely.

Social psychologists have studied several alternatives to the principle of procedural justice that have been posited to explain why people are liable both to accept as legitimate and to comply voluntarily with the regulations of authorities. Social exchange theories assume that people will accept decisions in a calculative way in order to maximize their outcomes. Distributive justice theories also emphasize outcomes, but focus on the fairness with which resources are distributed and the degree to which personal benefits are appropriate. Procedural justice theories also emphasize fairness, but instead of looking at outcomes, the judgment is made based on the degree to which the procedures used to reach the directives are consistent with the values of the group (Lind and Tyler, 1988, p. 222). After comparing these three principles, Tyler and Lind (1992, p. 163) conclude:

> In study after study, our research and that of other psychologists has shown that the favorability of a decision or even the fairness of the decision plays only a minor role in determining legitimacy. Much more important, it appears, are judgments of the fairness of the procedures. And judgments of procedural fairness are based, in turn, on process-based inferences about one's relationship with the authority. The belief that the authority views one as a full member of society, trust in the authority's ethicality and benevolence, and belief in the authority's neutrality—these appear to be the crucial factors that lead to voluntary compliance with the directives of authority.

Although much of the work done on procedural justice has been based on legal settings, Lind and Tyler (1988) have proposed that these processes operate in all societal settings. Procedural fairness is considered to be an antecedent to cooperative group behavior, which in turn makes groups more efficient and effective (Tyler and Blader, 2000).

Fairness of procedure has no objective criteria—it is what the members of the group believe it to be. Agreement on fairness comes from the processes of socialization through which group members come to share values and beliefs; new members of the group learn these values from the older members (Tyler, 1990). Students of governance have long recognized the value of fairness as an academic value, suggesting that good governance is based on "open plans, open policy statements, open findings, open reasons, open precedents, and fair informal and formal procedures" (Mortimer and Caruso, 1984). Any change in the faculty role in shared governance that is made without itself following the procedures of shared governance accepted by the faculty is likely to be considered procedurally unfair and therefore unacceptable.

Governance and Status

In *Leadership and Ambiguity*, Cohen and March (1974) proposed the simple hypothesis that "most people in a college are most of the time less concerned with the content of a decision than they are with eliciting an acknowledgment of their importance within the community. We believe that some substantial elements of the governance of universities can be better understood in terms of such a hypothesis than in terms of an assumption that governance is primarily concerned with the outcomes of decisions" (p. 121).

The structures and processes of shared governance identify the rights of the faculty to participate in making important decisions, thereby certifying their status and importance. People are concerned about their status in groups because high status within a valued group validates their own self-identity (Tyler and Lind, 1992). The importance of status in academic institutions can be gauged with a small thought experiment: faced with a choice between a promotion in rank with no salary increase, or a salary increase with no promotion, what proportion of faculty would choose the former over the latter?

Status, while important in its own right, is reinforced through its relationship to procedural justice because being treated fairly is, itself, a recognition of status. "To the extent that a procedure is seen as indicating a positive, full-status relationship, it is judged to be fair, and to the extent that a procedure appears to imply that one's relationship with the authority or institution is negative or that one occupies a low-status position, the procedure is viewed as unfair" (Tyler and Lind, 1992, p. 140). Perceptions of self-worth and perceptions of fairness are related; when one feels valued, one is also more likely to believe that the group is functioning effectively and fairly.

Governance and Social Capital

Reducing the faculty role in shared governance is likely also to inhibit the development of social networks and thereby reduce social capital. Academic institutions are rich in human capital because faculty and administrators are highly educated. At the same time, faculty autonomy, loose coupling, and the anarchical nature of academic institutions often means that colleges and universities are impoverished in terms of social capital. By increasing participation in governance activities, providing a sense of influence, and creating mixed senates, joint task forces, and other forums for interaction, shared governance is a means by which social capital may be created. In the same way, reducing opportunities for shared governance may also reduce social capital within an institution. Social capital is important because it leads to trust and cooperation; a reduction of social capital not only weakens the influence of constituents within an organization, but also reduces the effective influence of their leaders.

Social capital creates value by increasing the productivity of people in groups. According to Putnam (2000), "Social capital refers to connections among individuals—social networks and the norms of reciprocity and trustworthiness that arise from them. . . . Civic virtue is most powerful when embedded in a dense network of reciprocal social relations. A society of many virtuous but isolated individuals is not necessarily rich in social capital" (p. 19). Putnam supports his argument with a mass of data showing the relationship between indices of social capital and other desirable social outcomes. Among the reasons for these outcomes is that networks sustain rules of conduct and expectations of reciprocity that lead to trust, and a trustful society is more efficient than a distrustful one. Social capital makes it easier for constituents of a group to resolve collective problems, and the development of social networks provides the institutional means to encourage socially desirable behavior.

Trust between authorities and constituents can be developed when each believes that the other will act in a predictable way, and that each is concerned with and is able to act in the interests of the other. Trust strengthens the legitimacy of leaders and creates mutually reinforcing bonds of identity, confidence, and support between them. One of the main organizational consequences of trust is the willingness of constituents to comply voluntarily with the directives of authorities without needing to be offered rewards or threatened with punishment (Tyler, 1998). Trust is therefore an essential component of democratic governance that, without inducing alienation, leads to compliance and cooperation with the group. Trust in an authority can be based on that authority's ability to compete successfully for and allocate resources ("exchange trust," which is forward-looking), or it can be based on the ability to predict the authority's behavior because of a social connectedness that leads to shared norms and shared social identity ("communal trust," which is backward-looking) (Braithwaite, 1998). One consequence of communal, or social, trust is that it leads constituents to identify with the authority and to draw their identity from their work (Tyler, 1998). Communal trust depends on identification with the group and perceived agreement on common norms. Social trust is particularly important "within existing groups, in which social bonds are in place and people have already internalized group values" (Tyler, 1998, p. 287). If organizations that rely heavily on communal trust begin to give increased attention to exchange trust norms they may undermine the effectiveness of communal trust (Braithwaite, 1998).

Governing alone is like bowling alone—regardless of how wise or virtuous the person or office that determines what the rules should be, social capital within the group may not be increased and, in fact, is likely to be diminished as it transforms a process of reciprocal social interaction into an exercise in unilateral decision making. It is the process of shared governance, and not its outcome, that helps to build the dense network of connections that create social capital.

Conclusion

A number of generalizations can be drawn from the preceding concepts related to procedural justice, status, social capital, and social regulation.

Decisions made in social systems are more likely to be accepted when the procedures creating them are seen as legitimate and fair. What is considered fair is related to the expectations of people involved in the process, expectations that are learned through processes of socialization.

People are more likely to defer to the moral authority of structures and processes when they are developed so as to be consistent with existing social norms. Procedures or sanctions seen as illegitimate may lead not only to noncompliance, but to disrespect for the system that created them. Additional procedures, also seen as illegitimate, may be created to respond to noncompliance, thus reducing even further the influence of authorities.

Changes in social systems are more likely to be accepted when they do not challenge the social status of participants in that system and are less likely to be accepted when they do.

Systems that provide forums in which people can interact on matters related to their group norms and personal values help to create dense networks of interaction that increase social capital within the system. Higher levels of social capital, in turn, lead to increased trust and cooperation, which are related to organizational effectiveness.

Informal social controls may be more effective than formal legal controls in influencing social compliance with organizational values. The strength of these informal controls will decline as the frequency of interaction within organizations decreases.

Attempts to design utilitarian systems to increase organizational effectiveness may instead reduce effectiveness because they are inconsistent with participants' sense of what is proper.

In summary, normative, backward-looking processes may be more likely than utilitarian, forward-looking processes to support compliance in social systems, and they do this by increasing social capital and trust. The consequence is that rational processes meant to achieve specific outcomes in normative institutions are likely to be less effective than normative processes that are consistent with social norms and moral principles approved by the community. Utilitarian decisions may create rules, sanctions, and incentives, but since they are often not developed through legitimate processes and are often narrowly focused and difficult to enforce, they may decrease confidence in the system and increase alienation. The irony, as Robinson and Darley (1997) point out, is that while utilitarian approaches may appear to have some short-term benefits, normative approaches based on the values of social groups often turn out to be the most utilitarian.

Applying these ideas to academic institutions suggests that, since shared governance is a generally accepted normative principle, attempting to alter it by reducing the role of faculty is likely to have a number of predictable, and negative, consequences. Faculty members expect to play the preeminent role in issues related to the educational program and to have their voices heard on other important institutional matters, including those of governance itself. These expectations are inculcated during their professional socialization, reinforced by institutional history and academic tradition, articulated by respected leaders who reiterate the principle that the faculty must be involved in "developing and enforcing all the rules that protect academic values" (Bok, 2003, p. B9), and legitimated in authoritative documents such as the Joint Statement. Attempts to alter the faculty's role unilaterally will be seen as attacks on faculty status and will be considered illegitimate; shared norms will no longer provide a guide to behavior.

A further consequence is that the institution is likely to make less effective decisions. The three main parties to academic governance focus their attention on different things: trustees are concerned with responsiveness, administration with efficiency, and faculty with academic values. Each group has been socialized in different ways, is exposed to different aspects of the environment, has competence and expertise in different areas, and sees the institution from a unique perspective. Effective governance requires that the viewpoint of each group be considered in making decisions. In the words of W. H. Cowley, "academic governance is far too important to be left entirely in the hands of professors or entirely in the hands of boards of trustees. The enterprise requires the participation of both. . . . " (Wicke, 1963, p. 65).

In terms of the faculty role, shared governance is just another way of saying that those with expertise in an institution's core technology should have some important role in governing it. When that is not the case, "levels of satisfaction are likely to be low, the system may become too simple for its environment, problems are not properly attended to, and the institution may appear to lurch from crisis to crisis. . . . Governance systems that are not accepted by the parties lead almost inexorably to disruptive conflict" (Birnbaum, 1989, p. 39).

For all these reasons, changes in hard governance are unlikely to have the outcomes claimed for them. The configuration of hard governance itself, as long as it is accepted as legitimate by the participants, makes little difference because "governance guidelines in themselves have no animating power. In its most authentic sense, governance is simply the process by which people pursue common ends and, in the process, breathe life into otherwise lifeless forms. The best measure of the health of the governance structure at a college is not how it looks on paper, but the climate in which it functions" (Carnegie Foundation for the Advancement of Teaching, 1982, p. 88).

It is the climate of soft governance that encourages trust, which makes it more likely that constituents will be influenced by institutional norms and values without requiring formal rules and processes. Interaction and reciprocity build up the dense social networks that lead to trust among participants and to confidence in both the processes and the outcomes of the governance system (Del Favero, 2003). The best governance is invisible. If an institution spends inordinate time and energy on issues of governance, or must rely on hard governance to work, it is almost certainly not operating effectively.

The end of governance can only be to support the purposes of the institution that has created it. For market institutions, the purpose can be identified in terms of profit or some other quantifiable economic metric, and rational, forward-looking governance structures and processes may be quite effective. For academic institutions, however, the purpose is much less clear. These institutions are not concerned with profit, but with performance of mission; because that mission cannot be clearly articulated, the means to achieve it is always a matter of contention rather than certainty. These institutions may find the justification both for their mission, and for the governance systems that support it, by looking backward. "The university," said Emerson (1856), "must be retrospective. The gale that gives direction to the vanes on all its towers blows out of antiquity" (p. 882).

The purpose of academic institutions is not to create products but to embody ideas. Academic governance cannot be rationalized for the same reason that it is not possible to rationalize the purposes for which academic institutions exist. What kind of governance system can support academic institutions if their "ultimate business . . . is human freedom" (Bailey 1976, p. 76), if their task is "the creation of the future" (Whitehead, 1938, p. 233), if their aims are "wisdom and goodness" (Hutchins, 1943, pp. 23–24), and if it is (in Lord Haldane's words) "in universities that . . . the soul of a people mirrors itself" (Flexner, 1930, p. 186)? What rational processes can guide decisions if their purpose is, as John Stuart Mill had it, the "laying open to each succeeding generation . . . the accumulated treasure of the thoughts of mankind" (Garforth, 1971), if they are "the best and most benign side of our society insofar as that society aims to cherish the human mind" (Hofstadter, 1979, p. 38), and if they are to provide "a constant conversation . . . between past and present, a conversation the culture has with itself, on behalf of the country . . . making the world, for all its pain, work" (Giamatti, 1988, pp. 24–25)?

Lowell (1934, pp. 290–291), the president of Harvard, provided one backward-looking answer in 1920:

> The respective functions of the faculties and the governing boards—those things that each had better undertake, those it had better leave to the other, and those which require mutual concession—are best learned from experience and best embodied in tradition. Tradition has great advantages over regulations. It is a more delicate instrument; it accommodates itself to things that are not susceptible of sharp definition; it is more flexible in its application, making exceptions and allowances which it would be difficult to foresee or prescribe. It is also more stable. Regulations can be amended; tradition cannot, for it is not made, but grows, and can be altered only by a gradual change in general opinion, not by a majority vote. In short, it cannot be amended, but only outgrown.

Lowell recognized that the governance of an academic institution is organic, not mechanical. It is not designed so much as it evolves because it uniquely supports the activities of a social institution whose processes and goals cannot be clearly defined, whose outcomes cannot be precisely measured, but whose critical importance to society is indisputable. Proposals to improve governance by clarifying roles are as problematic as suggestions that institutions can become more effective by specifying outcomes. Both are likely to lead to increased bureaucratization, administrative influence, and the selection of data based on availability rather than on importance. Both are likely to strengthen hard governance at the expense of soft governance.

Governance is a means to an end. Therefore, the best forms of governance are those that evolve because they are most fit for a specific end. The calls for governance reforms that are more flexible and permit rapid decision making are rooted in classic notions of rationality and rational choice. The proponents of governance reform commonly take a forward-looking, utilitarian approach. Their arguments, however, are often based on ideology. As Enders (2002) writes, they "do not only or so much analyze reality but prescribe an ideal of 'good governance'" (p. 80). It is relatively easy to understand what they are against, but much more difficult to comprehend what they really want, and the system itself is so complex that the consequences of their recommendations cannot be predicted.

It is certain that academic institutions that remain true to their traditions to some extent will be responsive to contemporary pressures for economic or political relevance in the future as they have been in the past. However, they will not be as responsive as their critics demand. The fact that academic institutions cannot be expected to do everything is not necessarily bad. As Flexner (1930) pointed out, "universities that are held to their appropriate tasks will be unfit to do other things" (p. 27). Other institutions will be created to do what academic institutions should not. The competition of these new educational entities for resources should not be viewed as a threat, but as an opportunity for academic institutions to relieve themselves of programs and clienteles that are inappropriate to their purpose. Advocates for reform may argue that "faculty no longer can shut themselves off from the rest of society, as the commonly accepted notion of the ivory tower once implied" (Del Favero, 2003, p. 918). However, it is difficult to argue that, even when stressing its commitment to intellectual and personal development, academic institutions have ever been separated from the needs and interests of society, although there are disagreements about what those interests may be. Ivory towers have their place, and there are elements in higher education that cannot—and should not—be thought of as purely driven by society's manifest interests. After all, as Nisbet (1971) has argued, "What, in a civilized society, could possibly be wrong with, or stagnant, archaic, or antiquarian about, the vision of an enclave in the social order whose principal purpose is working creatively and critically with ideas through scholarship and teaching? Is not man's highest evolutionary trait thus far precisely his capacity for dealing with ideas: learnedly, imaginatively, and critically? Is there any more promising hallmark for a civilized society than its willingness to support a class of persons whose principal business is to think, to arrive at knowledge, and to induct others in this principal business?" (p. 208).

There is no crisis of governance among those institutions that emphasize academic as opposed to corporate values. Claims that such institutions are risking disruption or failure because they cannot respond quickly enough to a changing environment are both inaccurate and misplaced. It should not be surprising that such institutions are more stable and resistant to change than other kinds of organizations—indeed, that is what makes them institutions. And the older and more successful they are, the more difficult change will be. Because of the uncertainty of their technologies, universities have evolved so that their core activities are only loosely coupled to both their formal structure and their environment. One consequence is that they are less responsive to both administrative and political influence; the trade-off is that their core technologies can continue without disruption. The principles of shared governance enunciated in the 1967 Joint Statement continue to serve these institutions, and the larger society, well.

The crucial contemporary issue of governance, as Steck (2003) has pointed out, is to reclaim the traditional roles of academic institutions. "The core values and mission of the university must be sustained if the university is to fulfill its traditional role of learning, scholarship, and service. A fully corporatized university is only the shell of a university, and the task facing the academic community is to ensure that the inner core as well as the outer shell are preserved" (p. 81). This preservation will require that potential reform efforts "reflect upon histories as well as futures" (Gumport, 2000b, p. 87).

There is no doubt that, as its critics suggest, faculty participation in shared governance will have the effect of making it more difficult to change the programs and purposes of higher education. Whether this is a good thing or bad thing is a matter of ideology. The faculty are the primary upholders of the academic culture, so those that give precedence to the idea of a university as an academic institution—who believe with Masefield (1946, cited by Birnbaum, 2004, p. 19) that "there are few earthly things more splendid than a university"—are likely also to continue to believe in the importance of shared governance. The basic question to ask is not whether we want to make governance more efficient, but whether we want to preserve truly academic institutions. If the answer is affirmative, then shared governance is an essential precondition.

References

American Association of University Professors (AAUP). "Statement on Governance of Colleges and Universities, 1967." In *Policy Documents and Reports*. (9th ed.) Washington, D.C.: American Association of University Professors, 2001.

Association of Governing Boards of Universities and Colleges (AGB). *AGB Statement on Institutional Governance and Governing in the Public Trust; External Influences on*

Colleges and Universities. Washington, D.C.: Association of Governing Boards of Universities and Colleges, 2001.

Bailey, S. K. *The Purposes of Education.* Bloomington, Ind.: Phi Delta Kappa Educational Foundation, 1976.

Birnbaum, R. "Leadership and Followership: The Cybernetics of University Governance." In J. H. Schuster and others (eds.), *Governing Tomorrow's Campuses: Perspectives and Agenda.* Old Tappan, N.J.: Macmillan, 1989.

Birnbaum, R. *Management Fads in Higher Education.* San Francisco: Jossey-Bass, 2000.

Birnbaum, R. *Speaking of Higher Education.* Westport, Conn.: Praeger, 2004.

Blackburn, S. "Trust, Cooperation, and Human Psychology." In V. Braithwaite and M. Levi (eds.), *Trust and Governance.* New York: Russell Sage Foundation, 1998.

Bok, D. "Academic Values and the Lure of Profit." *Chronicle of Higher Education,* Apr. 4, 2003, pp. B7–B9.

Braithwaite, V. "Communal and Exchange Trust Norms: Their Value Base and Relevance to Institutional Trust." In V. Braithwaite and M. Levi (eds.), *Trust and Governance.* New York: Russell Sage Foundation, 1998.

Carnegie Foundation for the Advancement of Teaching. *The Control of the Campus.* Princeton, N.J.: Princeton University Press, 1982.

Cohen, M. D., and March, J. G. *Leadership and Ambiguity: The American College President.* New York: McGraw-Hill, 1974.

Cox, A. M. "Professors and Deans Praise Shared Governance, But Criticize Corporate Model." *Chronicle of Higher Education,* Nov. 17, 2000, p. A20.

Deal, T. E., and Kennedy, A. K. *Corporate Cultures: The Rites and Rituals of Organizational Life.* Reading, Mass.: Addison-Wesley, 1982.

Del Favero, M. "Faculty-Administrator Relationships as Integral to High-Performing Governance Systems." *American Behavioral Scientist,* 2003, *46*(7), 902–922.

Draper, A. S. "The University Presidency." *Atlantic Monthly,* 1906, *97,* 34.

Eckel, P. D. "Capitalizing on the Curriculum: The Challenges of Curricular Joint Ventures." In W. G. Tierney (ed.), *Academic Governance in a Protean Environment. American Behavioral Scientist,* 2003, *46*(7), 865–882.

Emerson, R. W. *English Traits.* New York: Routledge, 1856.

Enders, J. "Governing the Academic Commons: About Blurring Boundaries, Blistering Organisations, and Growing Demands." In *The CHEPS Inaugural Lectures 2002.* Enschede, The Netherlands: University of Twente, 2002.

Farrell, E. F. "Phoenix's Unusual Way of Crafting Courses." *Chronicle of Higher Education,* Feb. 14, 2003, p. A10.

Flexner, A. *Universities: American, English, German.* New York: Oxford University Press, 1930.

Garforth, F. W. *John Stuart Mill on Education.* New York: Teachers College Press, 1971.

Giamatti, A. B. *A Free and Ordered Space.* New York: Norton, 1988.

Gilmour, J. E., Jr. "Participative Governance Bodies in Higher Education: Report of a National Study." In R. Birnbaum (ed.), *Faculty in Governance: The Role of Senates and Joint Committees in Academic Decision Making.* New Directions for Higher Education, no. 75. San Francisco: Jossey-Bass, 1991.

Gumport, P. J. "Academic Governance: New Light on Old Issues." Occasional Paper no. 42. Washington, D.C.: Association of Governing Boards of Universities and Colleges, 2000a.

Gumport, P. J. "Academic Restructuring: Organizational Change and Institutional Imperatives." *Higher Education,* 2000b, *39,* 67–91.

Hofstadter, R. "Parting Shots: A Century of Commencement Speeches." *Saturday Review,* May 12, 1979, pp. 36–38.

Hutchins, R. M. *Education for Freedom.* Baton Rouge: Louisiana State University Press, 1943.

Ikenberry, S. O. "Mission and Market: A Leadership Struggle for Presidents." Presidential address at the annual meeting of the American Council on Education, Washington, D.C., Feb. 2001.

Kellogg Commission on the Future of State and Land-Grant Colleges. *Taking Charge of Change: Renewing the Promise of State and Land-Grant Universities.* Washington, D.C.: National Association of State Universities and Land Grant Colleges, 1996.

Kerr, C. *The Uses of the University.* Cambridge, Mass.: Harvard University Press, 1963.

Kerr, C. "Governance and Functions." *Daedalus,* 1970, 99(1), 108–121.

Kerr, C. "The Uses of the University Two Decades Later: Postscript 1982." *Change,* 1982, 14(7), 23–31.

Lind, E. A., and Tyler, T. R. *The Social Psychology of Procedural Justice.* New York: Plenum, 1988.

Lowell, A. L. *At War with Academic Traditions in America.* Cambridge, Mass.: Harvard University Press, 1934.

Mingle, J. R. "Higher Education's Future in the 'Corporatized' Economy." Occasional Paper no. 43, Washington, D.C.: Association of Governing Boards of Universities and Colleges, 2000.

Minor, J. T. "Assessing the Senate." *American Behavioral Scientist,* 2003, 46(7), 960–977.

Mortimer, K. P., and Caruso, A. C. "The Process of Academic Governance and the Painful Choices of the 1980s." In D. G. Brown (ed.), *Leadership Roles of Chief Academic Officers.* San Francisco: Jossey-Bass, 1984.

Nisbet, R. A. *The Degradation of the Academic Dogma.* New York: Basic Books, 1971.

Putnam, R. D. *Bowling Alone.* New York: Simon & Schuster, 2000.

Robinson, P. H., and Darley, J. M. "The Utility of Desert." *Northwestern University Law Review,* 1997, 91(2), 453–499.

Steck, H. "Corporatization of the University: Seeking Conceptual Clarity." *The Annals,* 2003, 585, 66–83.

Tappan, H. P. "The Idea of the True University." In R. Hofstadter and W. Smith (eds.), *American Higher Education: A Documentary History.* Chicago: University of Chicago Press, 1961.

Tyler, T. R. *Why People Obey the Law.* New Haven, Conn.: Yale University Press, 1990.

Tyler, T. R. "Trust and Democratic Governance." In V. Braithwaite and M. Levi (eds.), *Trust and Governance.* New York: Russell Sage Foundation, 1998.

Tyler, T. R., and Blader, S. L. *Cooperation in Groups: Procedural Justice, Social Identity, and Behavioral Engagement.* Philadelphia: Psychology Press, 2000.

Tyler, T. R., and Lind, E. A. "A Relational Model of Authority in Groups." *Advances in Experimental Social Psychology,* 1992, 25, 115–191.

Waugh, W. L., Jr. "Issues in University Governance: More 'Professional' and Less Academic." *The Annals,* 2003, 585, 84–96.

Whitehead, A. N. *Modes of Thought.* Old Tappan, N.J.: Macmillan, 1938.

Wicke, M. F. *Handbook for Trustees.* Nashville, Tenn.: Division of Higher Education, Board of Education, Methodist Church, 1963.

Yamada, M. "Joint Big Decision Committees and University Governance." In R. Birnbaum (ed.), *Faculty in Governance: The Role of Senates and Joint Committees in Academic Decision Making.* New Directions for Higher Education, no. 75. San Francisco: Jossey-Bass, 1991.

ROBERT BIRNBAUM *is Professor Emeritus of Higher Education at the University of Maryland, College Park.*

2

*Using national survey data, the author finds little
relationship between decision-making authority and the
actual decisions that are made.*

Do Governance Structures Matter?

Gabriel E. Kaplan

Much of the research on governance focuses on two apparent needs that are
often assumed to be conflicting: the need to preserve faculty authority and
influence, and the need for decision-making systems that respond efficiently
to change. Implicit in both of these needs is a presumption that governance
has a significant impact on decisions. Despite an extended body of policy
analysis and recommendations proceeding from this assumption, its underlying validity has rarely been examined or challenged.

This chapter examines the relationship between governance structures
and outcomes at a broad array of four-year institutions in the United States.
It reviews analysis of data drawn from a national Department of Education
survey of academic governance and outcomes. The paper finds few significant relationships between how governance organizes and vests authority,
on the one hand, and outcomes, on the other. In fact, the few significant
relationships that it does unearth challenge the expectations of models that
presume diverging interests between faculty, administrators, and boards.
The implications for future research are explored in conclusion.

Background

Governance refers to the means and actions by which a collective entity
decides matters of policy and strategy. Among scholars of higher education,
consideration of these processes and procedures of decision making take
precedence over the decisions themselves. In general, the governance system is understood to consist of the explicit and implicit procedures that
allocate to various participants the authority and responsibility for making
institutional decisions (Hirsch and Weber, 2001; Benjamin, 1993). In this

NEW DIRECTIONS FOR HIGHER EDUCATION, no. 127, Fall 2004 © Wiley Periodicals, Inc.

chapter, the focus is not on the culture of governance at a given institution, nor on the attitudes and norms suggesting how decisions ought to get made. Rather, my emphasis is on the actual decision-making structures that are chosen and how these structures relate to the implementation of decisions.

In higher education, the powers allocated to faculty, to the public's representatives, to students and parents, and to other participants vary greatly across public and private nonprofit institutions. There is extensive evidence that the ownership form of the institution significantly shapes its decisions (Kaplan, 2002a). Furthermore, there is evidence that, among public institutions, a great deal of the variance among outcomes is correlated with a state's systems for organizing public higher education (Kaplan, 2002a and 2002b; Lowry, 1998).

Do these differences persist at the institutional level? Do colleges and universities that vary in their decision-making structures also demonstrate predictable and patterned kinds of decisions? Can we identify the governance mechanisms that account for patterns of correlation? More specifically, do schools with representative senates tend to decide matters differently than schools in which all faculty members participate in a council? Do the decisions of schools in which the faculty has authority over one policy area differ much from schools where that authority rests with the administration? Typically, governance of higher education is subject to two kinds of criticisms. The first claims that academic governance has become too corporate and capitalistic and that decision-making models increasingly mimic the centralized powers of corporate management in the for-profit sector. The second criticism contradicts this view, arguing that shared governance is too arcane in its traditions and that it remains unresponsive to the economic pressures and demands of the modern world.

Unfortunately, such arguments circulate in an environment distinguished by a dearth of systematic and comprehensive information. Much that gets written about governance in higher education rests on anecdote or, at best, a handful of institutional case studies (Leslie, 1996). Although most studies in social science tend to be corroborative, negative findings can often be highly significant in policy analysis, influencing reform proposals that depend on untested assumptions and incomplete analysis. When it comes to governance, it would be most useful to know whether the various structures and systems that are in place yield varying outcomes.

This chapter seeks to fill the void in this area by reviewing survey data on governance structures. It singles out some of the findings of a comprehensive study of shared governance and its effects. It has been some time— roughly thirty years—since the last national efforts to collect governance data from a wide number of both public and private colleges and universities were completed (see American Association of University Professors (AAUP), 1971; Blau, 1973; Trow, 1977; and Ladd and Lipset, 1975). But in the past few years, several national studies have reinvestigated this issue (Kaplan, 2002a,

2002b, and 2004; Tierney and Minor, 2003). Such data allow us to look closely at both mechanisms of governance and allocations of power and authority. Combining this information with data on spending and resource allotment allows us to make inferences regarding the relationships between decision-making structures and organizational performance.

Hypotheses

The scope of the study that underlies this chapter goes beyond what is possible to cover in a short essay. The statistical results discussed here are available elsewhere, and those interested in the conclusions in full can find them by consulting the original research (see Kaplan, 2002b; Kaplan, 2003). Given the specific focus of this chapter, I will limit my discussion to findings in three areas: the significance of board structures, the role of faculty governing bodies, and the effects of vesting faculty with authority.

My investigation presumes that individuals are cognizant of their interests and seek to maximize their welfare within the constraints of their environment. Constraints come in various forms, but of particular interest here are the governance structures at a particular institution and how these structures distribute rights of decision making and participation among stakeholders. This rationalist approach draws heavily from what political economists have termed public choice or rational choice theory (McCubbins, Noll, and Weingast, 1989; Moe, 1990). It emphasizes that rules, procedures, and the assignment of authority play a key role in shaping the kinds of collective choices yielded by political structures. Much of this research has been confined to political bodies at the governmental level; rarely have its predictions been extended to the kinds of democratic participatory structures common at institutions of higher education (Lowry, 2001). When applied to the latter, rational choice theory presumes that such decision-making structures will shape the kinds of choices a school will make.

Governance structures in higher education can be said to matter in a predictive fashion only if they distinguish between faculty and other stakeholders, and only if stakeholder groups have divergent interests over certain issues. For instance, we might assume that, holding all other factors constant, faculty would have an interest in reducing teaching loads so they can focus on areas with more direct benefits, such as research. Lighter teaching loads, however, increase delivery costs and should be less desirable for both students and official overseers.

What components of the governance structure distribute authority in such a way that outcomes in specific areas will differ depending on who wields power? The corporate governance literature gives primacy to boards and the rules governing their function. Research in this area has focused on the size of boards, the rules of selection, the exclusion or inclusion of internal stakeholders, and the frequency of meetings (Blair, 1995; Lorsh, 1989).

In higher education, the governing board has a fiduciary duty to represent both the public's and the institution's interest. But because these interests are often ill-defined, boards delegate aspects of this authority to other parties. Nevertheless, the board's primacy suggests that reviewing the governing board policies is a vital aspect to understanding governance. This suggests the following hypothesis:

HYPOTHESIS 1. *Mechanisms that allocate board power to internal stakeholders will result in decisions that are favorable to faculty while those that allocate power to external stakeholders will yield decisions less favorable to faculty.*

The decisions that confront an institution at any given time can be broad and varied. Colleges and universities confront issues involving academic matters, financial planning and policy, and routine operations. Boards rarely retain authority and management responsibility over all of these areas. When boards delegate their authority to other stakeholders they have several options: they can decide which parties will have power over what areas, and they can also decide how formal that authority will be.

Regarding the first option, the assignment of authority over a particular area entails the allocation of power and, if actors pursue their interests, should yield outcomes favorable to those parties—or at least reflective of their interests and values. When administrators and boards guard their authority tightly, they help to move the institution in a direction far different from what might result if faculty were awarded more power. This suggests a second hypothesis:

HYPOTHESIS 2. *From a faculty perspective, more favorable outcomes in certain decisions will result when there is greater participation than when there is more limited involvement.*

Faculty participation, however, can take a variety of forms. Faculty can go about their jobs without formal day-to-day authority, intervening only when the party designated to decide a matter is perceived to overstep its bounds. When the designation of faculty authority is more formal and specific, the resulting structures elevate faculty power by creating procedural channels that must be followed, as well as by creating legally enforceable expectations about privileges and responsibilities (Weeks and Davis, 1982). Faculty power can become routinized and institutionalized, leading to an altered perception of who should be consulted on matters and whose opinions will count. This suggests a final hypothesis:

HYPOTHESIS 3. *More favorable outcomes for faculty will result from formalized systems of faculty influence in governance than from decision-making systems that devalue formal faculty participation.*

Data and Methods

My analysis used data that combined a national survey of governance structures with financial surveys compiled by the U.S. Department of Education (Computer-Aided Science Policy Analysis and Research (CASPAR), 1999; Kaplan, 2002a and 2002b). The former survey, the 2001 Survey of Higher Education Governance, was an effort to revisit and replicate earlier studies of governance while at the same time using contemporary work to formulate research questions that would shed light on current implementations of academic governance. The comprehensive data set that emerged from combining the governance survey with the Department of Education financial data allowed me to assess the correlation between the assignment of decision-making authority and the distribution of benefits such assignments produced.

Independent Variables. I used two econometric models that allowed me to control for institutional characteristics that could account for variation in higher education outcomes—characteristics such as the institution's mission, its public or private status, its possession (or lack of) a medical school, its selectivity, its insulation or dependence on the market, and the extent to which it was affected by regional differences. As experimental or control variables, the analysis focused on a large number of variables that record particular institutional features of the governance structure. Rather than discussing each variable here, I will analyze them within the context of the discussion regarding the results from each model.

Dependent Variables. In terms of dependent variables I focused on a number of institutional outcomes that are of interest to many observers of higher education, addressing in particular three areas: the president, finances, and strategic decisions.

The President. The survey provided data about the number of presidents each institution has had since 1970. Absent a more valid measure of institutional stability, this statistic provides an indication of the decision-making environment's volatility at a given institution and helps anticipate the possibility of gridlock among administrative and faculty stakeholders. The survey also recorded current presidents' professional backgrounds. Presidents who have a background in business or the military are often hired to import a different, more hierarchical ethic to the institution, while proponents of shared governance and faculty have traditionally favored leaders with a background in academia. Hence, the decision to hire a president with one background versus another can reveal stakeholder influence.

Institutional Finance. Few topics in higher education today draw as much attention and controversy as issues of finance (Selingo, 2003). Institutions are caught between the desires of parents, the public, and elected officials on the one hand (all of whom wish to keep operating costs and tuition low), and, on the other, the aspirations of faculty for more resources and improved financial rewards. The analysis used two measures of financial status—average faculty salaries and expenditures per student—to assess the role of governance in shaping institutional outcomes. Schools that spend more per student provide amenities with obvious rewards for faculty. Higher wages should also be seen as desirable.

Strategic Policy Decisions. From time to time institutions must decide whether to adopt the latest managerial innovations or change organizational routines. The survey data allowed me to assess the governance structures' relationship to decisions regarding program closure, adopting merit pay policies, or setting faculty teaching loads. Faculty with power should be interested in preventing the closure of programs and departments. Programs for competitive distribution of cost-of-living adjustments are viewed with hostility by unionized educators, and we might presume that faculty might be no different. And, all other things being equal, faculty should prefer lighter teaching loads. If governance structures significantly differ in the way they allocate power to stakeholders, then they might be expected to shape decisions in these matters.

Results

The results from the statistical models I ran provided only weak support at best for some kind of effect between the kinds of governance structures adopted and the results observed on campuses. The following three sections explain these findings with respect to the three preliminary hypotheses.

Board Policies. Theories about effective board practices suggest a number of independent variables to explore how board structures influence outcomes in higher education. For instance, research on corporate governance has argued for limitations on board size in order to render board processes more coherent and effective. Boards that meet more frequently are better able to monitor their managerial agents. Research has called for excluding internal stakeholders such as employees from board membership so that boards do not neglect their fiduciary duties in favor of a particular group. Properly insulated boards, then, are expected to select their own members and preserve their disinterested position. Self-perpetuating boards are likely to be more homogeneous and consistent. Members selected by the governor are likely to be more attuned to public sensibilities; that is, these members are likely to push an institution away from academic norms and toward those more common among the general populace. My analysis, therefore, encompassed the rules surrounding governing board composition, board size, meeting frequency, selection mechanisms, and faculty, student, and administrator representation.

None of the board policies were associated with greater turnover in executive leadership. Nor were they associated with either an increase or reduction in teaching loads. Vesting internal stakeholders with a role in board selection increased the likelihood of an academic president at the helm and reduced the likelihood of program closure, but this was the only board policy that had any significant effect on these decisions. None of the other aspects of board composition—including faculty participation in board activities—seemed to matter.

Larger boards were associated with a modest increase in faculty salaries, but faculty membership on the board was associated with lower salaries. None of the other practices had any significant relationship to wages. Only in the area of total expenditures were board practices noteworthy, and here again the direction of these effects went against expectations. Self-perpetuating boards tended to spend more money, not less, than boards appointed by external agents and boards selected by internal stakeholders. Student membership on the board was associated with higher expenditures and operating costs, while faculty membership was associated with lower expenditures. This suggests that faculty membership may be used as a remuneration strategy to compensate faculty who are likely to experience lower levels of pay and fewer professional amenities.

Apart from these findings, the most significant result was how few of the variables proved to be significant in the models. Out of nine econometric models, three indicated that only one board policy was significant in its effects, and two indicated that no characteristics were significant in shaping outcomes. Even in the area of expenditures, more than half of the board practice variables had little effect on outcomes.

The Allocation of Influence and Authority. The new governance survey drew questions from its thirty-year-old predecessor; the older survey had broken faculty influence into five categories, asking respondents to use these categories to classify faculty participation in fifteen decision-making areas (American Association of University Professors, 1971). Both surveys indicated that faculties tend to have significant responsibility for academic and appointment matters, and that they tend to be less involved in matters of financial and institutional planning. And the responses to the survey questions tended to be uniform across the educational sector, regardless of size, ownership form, and even mission.

Using those responses, the analysis assessed the relationship between the fraction of faculty with significant influence in a given area and the outcomes surrounding the presidency, institutional finance, and strategic planning. The findings suggested that faculty participation and influence in governance was only modestly related to institutional outcomes. The proportion of faculty participation in all examined areas had no relationship to the likelihood of program closure or of a president with a background in academia. In five other models, there was only one area in which faculty involvement proved to affect outcomes. Greater faculty participation in appointments was associated with an increased likelihood that the institution adopted merit pay policies. Greater faculty involvement in decisions about construction was associated with lower levels of per-student expenditures. Faculty involvement in the appointments of deans was correlated with lower rather than higher faculty salaries—although this effect was limited. Despite the perception that faculty would be inclined to push for institutional expansion, the evidence here supports the notion that faculty interests may lie in other areas.

Unsurprisingly, perhaps, faculty participation in setting average teaching loads was associated with lower teaching loads. However, this was the only decision area in which faculty involvement appeared to affect teaching loads. Only with respect to the issue of faculty salaries did faculty participation in several decision-making areas appear to be important. Faculty involvement in faculty appointments was positively associated with faculty salary levels. Faculty involvement in setting salary scales appeared to be associated with higher faculty salaries. Nevertheless, these effects remained quite small. Overall, the effects from involving faculty in decision-making areas around academics, finance, and operations were rather modest.

Institutional Practices of Shared Governance. A third set of evaluative models examined the role formal and informal structures played in enabling faculty to participate in governance. One set of variables recorded whether the locus of faculty authority was at the departmental level, the division level (such as college or school), the institution-wide level, or the union level. The level at which faculty influence operates may indicate the degree to which decisions are decentralized. If Massy and Zemksy (1997) are correct, decentralization of decision making at the departmental level is one of the mechanisms responsible for ratcheting up costs. Another set of variables recorded whether the institution had a faculty senate, a campus senate for its stakeholders, full meetings of the faculty, or divisional units of governance.

Responses in this area provide an indication of the formality of faculty governance and the weight of faculty voices relative to those of other participants. Formal decision-making structures might be expected to be more facile and less parochial in nature, while those with a broader range of participants might be less focused on faculty-specific concerns.

A third set of variables assessed the administration's role in the faculty governance body, since defenders of shared governance argue that administrative participation can potentially inhibit faculty expression (AAUP, 1995). Finally, the models employed variables that recorded how survey respondents characterized the faculty's role in governance. Respondents could characterize faculty as playing an advisory role, a policy-influencing role, or a direct policymaking role. Once again, in six of the models, only one measure proved to be significantly related to an outcome. The level at which faculty most directly influenced an institution's governance—department, division, campus, or union—proved to be insignificant in all of the models. The number of presidents in the last thirty years was unrelated to all of the factors that captured the formality of faculty governance. Full faculty meetings were associated with lower faculty salary levels, while academic senates were associated with lower expenditures. In governance bodies that operated at the division level, it was less likely that the president came from academia and more likely that a school adopted merit pay. The only results that fit neatly with the expectations of the rationalist hypotheses were in the area of decisions about teaching loads and program closures. The latter were more likely if the faculty role in governance was weaker. Closures were least likely when faculty played a direct role in policymaking. An academic senate was associated with lower teaching loads. However, if the president had authority to chair the faculty governance body, this also was associated with a reduced teaching load. Despite the fears of some that administrative participation in governance weakens faculty voice, the findings here appear to suggest otherwise. In no case was administrative participation in governance associated with outcomes faculty might view less favorably.

Once again, the most striking results from this analysis echoed the earlier findings. Few of the variables proved to be significantly associated with the outcomes measured here. Of the variables tested, roughly 87 percent proved to be insignificant.

Discussion

The findings from this study demonstrate only a moderate relationship between institutional decisions and the assignment of authority for those decisions. Faculties with significant authority appeared to be no more likely than administrators with significant authority to make self-interested decisions. The research also found little relationship between governance structures—such as faculty senates, academic senates, faculty advisory councils, and others—and the decisions that institutions subsequently implemented. Salaries, teaching loads, financial health, and expenditures appeared to have only a small correlation with structures of governance and the relative influence of parties. But the scope and consistency of these effects was slight. If faculty influence over policy had only a small effect on outcomes, faculty participation on the board was associated with lower wages and expenditures.

Two major points seem clear from this analysis. First, structures of governance do not appear to account, in a significant way, for variance in outcomes among institutions of higher education. Second, where effects could be observed, they often ran counter to predictions based both on the self-interested behavior and conflicting interests of all groups, and on models of adversarial relations among faculty, boards, and administrators. For instance, where faculty control could be observed, it was related to lower wages and expenditures and higher teaching loads. Administrative influence—such as giving a president voting rights on the board—was associated with higher levels of expenditures. Self-perpetuating boards may have been more favorably disposed to merit pay programs but they were also associated with higher expenditure levels.

These findings suggest several possibilities. First, explicit forms of governance may not matter that much. Despite our current preoccupation with getting structures of governance right, the rewards for altering structure are not likely to be as radical as models developed in political economy would suggest. Our concern for and focus on governance structures may be misplaced, or at least overemphasized.

Second, outcomes in higher education may be more significantly related to factors beyond structural arrangements. Resource dependency theory suggests that it is the composition of external resources that matters here. Resource flows may lead to a divergence between explicit authority (that is, the vested right to make a decision), and actual power (the ability to influence the decision taken) (Pfeffer and Salancik, 1978).

Another possibility is that cultural conditions specific to a campus may trump structural arrangements. Gumport's work on retrenchment (1993) highlights the idea that governance may or may not be important in outcomes. In her analysis, the governance structure mattered on one campus where faculty were able to use governance structures to voice opinion and influence outcomes. But on another campus, the governance structure was not used as a vehicle for redressing grievances about program termination and department closures. Because faculty and administrators on this second campus were not uniformly opposed to each other, faculty in one area of a school could side with the administration rather than with the colleagues whose programs were threatened. Gumport's study showed that the fault lines were not between faculty and administrators, but between those aligned with national science policy, who possessed political power—and connections to resources—and those who were not so aligned.

What seems clear is that mechanisms of governance by themselves do not necessarily empower one group to bend the institution toward purposes that are uniformly held across that group. Faculty interests and views are likely to be as diverse among themselves as they are between faculty and administrators. Similarly, administrators and administrative interests are not more likely to be uniformly oriented toward budget containment, efficiency, and cost minimization. In other words, instead of trying to understand the effects of these groups individually, a more useful focus of research, policy analysis, and implementation might be on process writ large. The implicit understandings shared by parties in governance animate and give life to the structures of decision making. Where faculty, boards, and administrators all share the same values, institutions are likely to pursue the same policies regardless of who wields the greatest power. It is not, then, structures such as the faculty senate that give voice to the faculty. Rather, it is a commitment on the part of administrators and boards to hear the voice of the faculty. When values are not aligned, then the board may assert its prerogatives regardless of faculty sentiment, ignoring the structures that give voice to faculty sentiments.

None of the variables collected in the survey provide an accurate assessment of institutional values, norms, and commitments to particular traditions and processes. It is not possible, therefore, to corroborate the above suggestion. However, the failure to corroborate our expectations regarding the role of structures suggests that a more fruitful avenue for future research on governance would be to explore the processes by which institutions engage the structures that they have in place. My hunch is that the guiding force in the implementation of shared governance is institutional culture, along with the geniality or hostility of the surrounding environment.

References

American Association of University Professors (AAUP). "Report of the Subcommittee of Committee T." *AAUP Bulletin,* 1971, 57(1), 68–124.

American Association of University Professors. *Policy Documents and Reports* (8th ed.) Washington, D.C.: American Association of University Professors, 1995.

Benjamin, R. *The Redesign of Governance in Higher Education.* Santa Monica, Calif.: Rand, 1993.

Blair, M. *Ownership and Control: Rethinking Corporate Governance for the Twenty-First Century.* Washington, D.C.: Brookings Institution, 1995.

Blau, P. M. *The Organization of Academic Work.* (2nd ed.) New York: Transaction, 1973.

Computer-Aided Science Policy Analysis and Research (CASPAR). Washington, D.C.: National Science Foundation. Updated Sept. 15, 2003, http://caspar.nsf.gov/. Accessed Aug. 1999.

Gumport, P. J. "The Contested Terrain of Academic Program Reduction." *Journal of Higher Education,* 1993, 64(3), 283–311.

Hirsch, W. Z., and Weber, L. (eds.). *Governance in Higher Education: The University in a State of Flux.* Paris: Economica Ltd., 2001.

Kaplan, G. E. "Results from the 2001 Survey on Higher Education Governance: Sponsored by the American Association of University Professors and the American Conference of Academic Deans." Updated Jan. 2002. http://www.ksg.harvard.edu/2001survey/2001%20Governance%20Survey%20Results.pdf. Accessed May 15, 2003.

Kaplan, G. E. "When Agents Seem to Have No Principles: Resource and Benefit Allocation in Public and Nonprofit Institutions of Higher Education." Unpublished paper, John F. Kennedy School of Government, Harvard University, 2002a.

Kaplan, G. E. "Between Politics and Markets: The Institutional Allocation of Resources in Higher Education." Unpublished doctoral dissertation, Faculty of Graduate School of Arts and Sciences, Harvard University, 2002b.

Kaplan, G. E. "Extending Public Choice Theory to Non-Governmental Democratic Structures of Decision: The Case of Higher Education." Unpublished paper, Graduate School of Public Affairs, University of Colorado, 2003.

Kaplan, G. E. "How Academic Ships Actually Navigate: A Report from the 2001 Survey on Higher Education Governance." In R. G. Ehrenberg (ed.), *Governing Academia.* Ithaca, N.Y.: Cornell University Press, 2004.

Ladd, E. C., and Lipset, S. *The Divided Academy: Professors and Politics.* New York: McGraw-Hill, 1975.

Leslie, D. W. "Review Essay: Strategic Governance: The Wrong Questions?" *Review of Higher Education,* 1996, 20(1), 101–112.

Lorsch, J. W. *Pawns or Potentates: The Reality of America's Corporate Boards.* Boston: Harvard Business School Press, 1989.

Lowry, R. C. "Mission, Governance Structure and Outcomes at Quasi-Autonomous Public Institutions: Evidence for American Universities." Paper presented at the Annual Meeting of the American Political Science Association, Boston, Sept. 3, 1998.

Lowry, R. C. "Governmental Structure, Trustee Selection, and Public University Prices and Spending: Multiple Means to Similar Ends." *American Journal of Political Science,* 2001, 45(4), 845–861.

Massy, W. F., and Zemsky, R. "A Utility Model for Teaching Load Decisions in Academic Departments." *Economics of Education Review,* 1997, *16*(4), 349–365.

McCubbins, M. D., Noll, R. G., and Weingast, B. R. "Structure and Process, Politics, and Policy: Administrative Arrangements and the Political Control of Agencies." *Virginia Law Review,* 1989, *75,* 431–482.

Moe, T. M. "The Politics of Bureaucratic Structure." In J. E. Chubb and P. E. Peterson (eds.), *Can the Government Govern?* Washington, D.C.: Brookings Institution, 1990.

Pfeffer, J., and Salancik, G. R. *The External Control of Organizations: A Resource Dependence Perspective.* New York: HarperCollins, 1978.

Selingo, J. "House Republicans Issue Scathing Report on College-Cost 'Crisis.'" *Chronicle of Higher Education,* Sept. 12, 2003, p. A20.

Tierney, W. G., and Minor, J. T. *Challenges for Governance: A National Report.* Los Angeles: Center for Higher Education Policy Analysis, University of Southern California, 2003.

Trow, M. A. *Aspects of American Higher Education, 1969–1975.* Berkeley, Calif.: Carnegie Council on Policy Studies in Higher Education, 1977.

Weeks, K. M., and Davis, D. (eds.). *Legal Deskbook for Administrators of Independent Colleges and Universities.* (2nd ed.) Washington, D.C.: National Association of College and University Attorneys and Waco, Tex.: Center for Constitutional Study, Baylor University, 1982.

GABRIEL E. KAPLAN *is assistant professor of public affairs at the University of Colorado's Graduate School of Public Affairs in Denver, Colorado.*

3

Changing structures may be a less important factor in creating an effective approach to governance than leadership, relationships, and trust.

What Is More Important to Effective Governance: Relationships, Trust, and Leadership, or Structures and Formal Processes?

Adrianna Kezar

Over the past several decades, there has been considerable criticism about academic governance within institutions of higher education. A national study in the 1990s found that 70 percent of campus faculty, staff, and administrators believed that decision-making processes were working ineffectively, and noted that new approaches needed to be considered (Dimond, 1991). Some posit that academic governance limits an institution's agility and flexibility, creating obstructions and sluggishness, and fostering a predisposition toward the status quo (Association of Governing Boards of Universities and Colleges, 1996; Schuster, Smith, Corack and Yamada, 1994). Others worry that administrators have become fixated on meeting political and social pressures, stabilizing finances, and promoting efficiency and accountability; the problem, according to this view, is that these administrators have also lost touch with education-based decision making, quality, and the real purposes of higher education (Birnbaum, 1989; Tierney, 2000). There is widespread acknowledgment of the governance problem, but few solutions have been proposed and, of those, few have proven successful.

The dominant perspective, or common wisdom, is that campus governance needs radical alteration of its structure and its formal processes. One well-publicized study by Benjamin and Carroll of the RAND Corporation (1998) suggested that campus governance was wholly ineffective and

New Directions for Higher Education, no. 127, Fall 2004 © Wiley Periodicals, Inc.

inefficient because of its structure and processes. The authors found that campus governance structures and processes do not allow for timely review or for effective, expertise-based decision making; furthermore, they are not responsive to external concerns.

In the midst of these calls to reform governance radically through restructuring, a second perspective is emerging—one that suggests that relationships, trust, and leadership, rather than reengineering, are key to enhancing governance (Braskamp and Wergin, 1998; Del Favero, 2003; Weingartner, 1996). This perspective is described by Robert Birnbaum's meta-analysis, *Management Fads in Higher Education* (2000). Birnbaum demonstrates that restructuring and reengineering have failed to bring the improvements that were claimed for them. Instead, Birnbaum suggests, enhancing leadership, developing training, and building relationships might be more effective methods for improving institutional operations.

This emerging perspective has not yet been articulated in a comprehensive way. Instead, scholarly work on leadership, relationships, and trust has occurred in isolated pockets across the discipline. In this chapter, drawing on both previous and current research, I bring these independent voices together to articulate a unified counternarrative to the structural view of how to improve governance.

What Are Governance and Effectiveness?

Governance refers to the process of policymaking and macrolevel decision making within higher education. At the broadest level, the literature on governance has typically examined state boards, boards of trustees, faculty senates, and student government. This chapter focuses on academic (or internal) governance, which is defined as the manner in which issues affecting the entire institution (or one or more components thereof) are decided (Lee, 1991).

A few authors have offered definitions of effectiveness or good governance. Schuster, Smith, Corak, and Yamada (1994) suggested that effectiveness is the value of achieving a quality decision and that it is based on competence. Further, there are some generally accepted principles when it comes to quality: quality is defined in terms of outcomes; quality involves integrity of process; and quality requires decisions based on evidence, wherever possible (Massey, 2003).

Birnbaum (1991a) offered a different definition of good or effective governance, one that is tied directly to the culture of individual institutions. Birnbaum notes that as each college or university varies in its definition of effectiveness, generalizations are difficult to make. However, he notes that effectiveness is a match between the expectations of constituents and how the process and outcomes evolve. Therefore, if people on campus believe in a political process based on negotiation and compromise, then governance is effective if its process and outcomes reflect that approach. Birnbaum's work suggests that structures would be important on bureaucratic campuses or within bureaucratic units of a campus, whereas relationships would be more important on small, collegial campuses. In addition, definitions of effectiveness vary depending on whether a campus is bureaucratic (stressing efficiency) or political (stressing interest group contentment).

Schuster's and Birnbaum's definitions of effectiveness are both helpful. Campus culture matters and, at certain institutions, either structures or informal political processes will likely take on greater importance. Still, certain conditions that facilitate governance may transcend cultures altogether. The most important ones, in my view, are leadership, relationships, and trust.

Interrelationship of Structures and Process with Leadership and Relationships

In this chapter, I examine structures and formal processes, artificially separating them from relationships and leadership. I make this distinction only to emphasize where institutions may want to focus efforts and resources. For example, it can be expensive both to alter a governance structure radically and to provide leadership training. Institutions will not always have the luxury, especially in these difficult financial times, to pay for both. It is important to note that structures and processes tend to influence relationships, leadership arrangements, and trust. For instance, if faculty and administrators develop a process to ensure consultation and the advice produced by that consultation is used, trust is developed.

Similarly, but perhaps less formally, relationships and leadership can have an effect on structures and processes. In this way structures and processes begin to look different in practice than they do on paper. For example, a committee might begin with a specific charge, timeline, and set of procedures, yet through conversations the charge might be modified, new people might be added to the committee, and meeting procedures might be altered. In other words, structures and processes are not static. Still, in this essay I separate structures and processes from leadership and relationships as a heuristic device that enables us to examine how to create effective governance and advise about where to focus efforts. Structures and processes as well as relationships and leadership are important for any governance process.

In addition, policymakers and leaders are usually inclined toward global, singular solutions that involve restructuring. Working with individual people and developing relationships can be a more arduous, unpredictable, and long-term task. In the rush for quick-fix solutions, institutions grasp for scientific management techniques that tend to focus more on structure and process than on people and relationships. Because of this bias among policymakers and leaders, it is important to explore alternative methods for creating meaningful change within academic governance.

The Conventional Wisdom: Change Structures and Governance Will Be More Effective

Scholars utilizing structural theories suggest that the most important aspect in creating a functional governance system is to focus on organizational structures such as lines of authority, roles, procedures, and bodies responsible for decision making. Scholars also study structure because they believe that it can be "managed" or altered more directly than social interaction, which it nevertheless influences. This research is appealing because it provides a clear roadmap for policymakers. The appeal is clear—but does it work?

Although governance is an understudied area (see Kezar and Eckel, forthcoming), the limited research that has been done focuses on structure. The majority of this work suggests that structure has an impact on efficiency but does little to improve effectiveness. For example, studies find that the size and complexity of the governance structure or process affects the efficiency of decision making; the larger the size of the institution, the more time-consuming the process will be (Birnbaum, 1991b; Cohen and March, 1974; Lee, 1991; Mintzberg, 1979). The composition and role of governance bodies also influence efficiency (Dill and Helm, 1988; Lee, 1991). If the governance body includes key individuals with the necessary expertise and a clear understanding of their role, then the process becomes more efficient (Dill and Helm, 1988).

In terms of effectiveness, however, structural approaches have proven more limited (for a detailed description of this issue, see Kezar and Eckel, forthcoming). It is true that better-articulated structures—such as committees with clear charges and defined roles—can shape effectiveness (Mortimer and McConnell, 1979; Schuster, Smith, Corak, and Yamada, 1994). And lack of rewards for participation in governance shapes both effectiveness (not attracting strong people to these roles on campus) and efficiency, in that people make governance a low priority as a result (Dill and Helm, 1988; Gilmour, 1991; Mortimer and McConnell, 1979).

Still, most studies of governance structures have been limited in scope (examining one or two structural modifications) and small in size (a few case studies, or surveys of a limited number of institutions). A recent comprehensive study (involving a survey of several thousand institutions and multiple structural variables) by Kaplan (Chapter Two, this volume) helps to provide even more definitive evidence that structures are not meaningful to governance. Kaplan examined board size, meeting frequency, allocation of board power, union status, centralization and decentralization, and other structural issues, and studied how they related to a set of governance outcomes or policies, like merit pay or teaching loads. In the end, Kaplan found only a small relationship between decisions that are arrived at and structural issues like the assignment of authority over those decisions. He notes that "structures of governance do not appear to account, in a significant way, for variance in outcomes among institutions of higher education" (p. 31).

These findings would not be surprising to organizational scholars, who have demonstrated that organizations generally do not operate as bureaucracies in which structure accounts for behavior. Instead, organizations are political, relational, and anarchical.

Recent Wisdom: Leadership and Relationships

It is somewhat problematic to describe scholarship on leadership and relationships as "recent wisdom"; insights on these topics should rather be considered old wisdom that has had a rebirth recently, challenging the bureaucratic and scientific views of organizations that have been prevalent over the last hundred years. Morgan (1997) attributes the reemerging emphasis on humanity within organizations to the development of human relations, as well as cultural and political theories of organization. However, none of these theories were able to rival the hold of structural perspectives until breakthroughs in the natural sciences demonstrated that the physical universe operates in more organic, interconnected ways than was previously supposed. Most of the recent literature on organizations (chaos theory, for instance) highlights that relationships are more important than structures and processes because organizations must be able to alter structures and processes to adapt to circumstances. In other words, structures and processes are not the heart of organizations—people and relationships are (Wheatley, 1996). As Del Favero (2003) notes, organizations thrive only to the extent that participant relationships are central to decision-making processes.

In addition to the newer theories of organizations, which emphasize the significance of relationships to organizational performance and functioning, earlier research on governance provides evidence that conventional wisdom about structures is off the mark. Schuster, Smith, Corak, and Yamada (1994) demonstrated that leadership and leadership style are critical to governance outcomes; in fact, of all the conditions examined in that study, leadership and leadership style had the most significant impact on governance effectiveness. In their analysis of ten institutions, Schuster, Smith, Corak, and Yamada determined that efficiency, implementability, and ownership of the governance process were strongly related to leadership. Middle-level leadership among faculty senate committee chairs, chairs, deans, and faculty was found to be the most important to creating effective governance. Lee (1991) and Birnbaum (1991b) demonstrated that the quality of senate leadership affected administrators' perceptions of whether the group was effective. Lee also found that campuses that addressed leadership continuity and provided information, training, and advice to new officers were more successful at governance. However, orientation and development of leaders within governance was uncommon; few campuses provided these opportunities (Birnbaum, 1991b; Lee, 1991).

Several studies have found that interpersonal dynamics, group processes, group motivation and interest, and committee membership are among the most significant issues that campuses should focus on in order to improve governance (Baldridge, 1971 and 1982; Birnbaum, 1991b; Dill and Helm, 1988; Mortimer and McConnell, 1979; Schuster, Smith, Corak, and Yamada, 1994). Yet most of these studies did not focus on relationships in much depth. An exception is a case study analysis by Lee (1991) that focused on academic senates. She found that informal interaction—interaction outside the hierarchical structure and beyond designated roles—was critical to success. She further identified that certain relationships were particularly critical; for example, interpersonal dynamics between the president and the senate chair are instrumental to the success or failure of governance.

The focus of such studies has been on means for increasing participation and on consultation as a proxy for relationships. In other words, consultation is seen as inherently relational and important to the development of the sorts of interpersonal connections that might be sustained over time. Mortimer and McConnell (1979) conducted an extensive case study analysis to determine the most important aspects of a functional governance system; they found that having healthy relationships was critical. These relationships are developed through participation and consultation. In addition, a more inclusive process with broad participation increases the likelihood of valuable input that can improve a policy or decision (Williams, Gore, Broches, and Lostski, 1987). The major components of the consultation process include early input, joint formulation of procedures, adequate time to articulate responses, availability of information, adequate feedback, and communication of decisions (Dill and Helm, 1988). Participation and consultation alone are not adequate to build relationships, but being able to see that input has altered decisions or been taken into consideration is necessary for involvement to be considered legitimate. These kinds of interactions lead to greater commitment and, over time, to greater effectiveness and efficiency (Lee, 1991; Dimond, 1991).

The notion of legitimacy in relationships relates to issues of trust. Lee's case study of three campuses found that a history of mistrust between faculty and administrators had an impact on the success of governance at those institutions. Governance effectiveness has been demonstrated to be related to accountability on the part of the ultimate decision makers, and the sense that they listen to the council or senate, or whatever governance bodies exist on campus (Lee, 1991; Schuster, Smith, Corak, and Yamada, 1994). The importance of trust is also confirmed by studies that illustrate that governance processes have been brought to a halt when feedback is not followed or commitments are otherwise broken (Lee, 1991; Schuster, Smith, Corak, and Yamada, 1994). Although our knowledge on these issues is still limited, there is evidence to support the importance of leadership, relationships, and trust to a robust governance process.

In summary, restructuring and other structural solutions have had a significant effect on efficiency but minimal impact on effectiveness. In contrast, previous research has demonstrated that leadership, relationships, and trust have strong potential for increasing effectiveness. The few existing studies on relationships, leadership, and trust have rarely provided sufficient depth to understand why these concepts and conditions are so important and how they are related to effectiveness. The case study project described below adds greater depth of understanding about why these three elements are so meaningful for creating effective governance.

Stories from Campuses with New Approaches to Governance

The stories in this section are taken from case studies of campuses that have altered their governance process. These stories are useful because they demonstrate what it is like to address a governance system that is not working. Initially, each campus had altered the structure of governance, but had not focused on relationships, trust, or leadership in relation to it. This is not unusual, of course. As noted earlier, almost all campuses are guided by conventional wisdom, and thus are inclined to alter structures when dealing with governance problems. In these case studies, I examined what emerged as more important for making governance systems effective. Effectiveness was determined according to campus participants' perceptions as well as the researchers' observations. The case studies involved interviews with faculty, staff, and administrators. Prior to visiting each campus, I reviewed planning documents for the change in governance, evaluation of the governance system, faculty senate reports, institutional planning documents, task force and committee reports, and accreditation reports.

The stories and examples supported the second perspective emerging in the literature; that is, that what really matters for governance is leadership, relationships, and trust. On campuses where these three elements were missing, governance was not effective, regardless of the structures present. In turn, no matter how problematic the structures, if these elements existed, governance was generally effective. These examples are helpful for understanding some of the ways that these elements made a significant difference.

Leadership as Pivotal. New structures were only as successful as the leaders that emerged on campuses. Structures alone could not facilitate effective decisions and policymaking. Campuses that had poor leadership around governance failed, while dedicated leaders (or groups of leaders) made the new structures work. Leadership facilitated effectiveness by providing a sense of direction and priorities and moving processes toward an outcome. People involved in governance noted that you can have the right individuals involved and the correct type and size of teams, but without a person to drive the process, policymaking will stall or be misdirected to minutiae. Several people on one campus described the apt work of a participatory faculty leader and how she created direction, pointing out that "She kept us thinking about the big picture, moved conversations along, and was organized." Most people said this particular leader was unique because she had administrative and leadership training and experience.

Consistently, individuals serving on effective governing bodies described a leader (or group of leaders) who provided direction, movement, and priorities. Leadership styles varied—some were participatory and some were directive—but regardless of style, campus participants reflected on the importance of providing direction and being focused on outcomes. Leadership was not always traceable to a single individual; it might come from cochairs or a subset of the senate. In addition, leadership sometimes emerged among individuals without positions of power (for example, the senate chair of vice presidents). Instead, a new faculty member in, say, math might lead the charge on an issue. One person described how one task force member helped create an effective process: "I have been on too many groups that floundered in discussion. Harry just took it on to provide that focus for our group. He provided vision and also guided discussion." The existence of many informal leaders also demonstrates how the development of formal processes and structures cannot ensure leadership.

A sense of direction led to greater involvement and commitment from participants—particularly key individuals with legitimacy and status on campus. A faculty leader described her success at getting numbers of expert members on her governing unit; critical to quality decision making, such membership was also rare: "I think it's one of the reasons we don't have difficulty getting people to serve on that group. I spoke with somebody who had been on Y who put his name in as a nominee for X and he said, 'One of the reasons I did it is because you people get things done, I trust the leadership.'"

Although these two committees had identical structures, they had different leadership; it was the leadership that people believed created a more effective process (both because it provided the direction and priorities for the committee and because it involved key people) and thus resulted in better decisions.

As involvement and commitment of key people increased, so did ownership and a sense of meaning. Governance was no longer a task or routine activity that people had to "suffer" through to meet institutional obligations or to prevent poor decisions that jeopardized work conditions and student learning. Instead, governance became an activity that participants could see meaningfully shaping their environment and creating an effective context for learning as well as a thriving institution. This was a critical turn that leadership was instrumental in creating. The story of a particular committee on one campus demonstrates how a leader facilitated this change by giving a short speech about the contributions of the committee. The leader then asked people to reflect on what they felt they had accomplished; she was amazed that they didn't speak about specific goals, but that instead "what came out was a real sense of appreciation that this was not another committee, it was a group that had made meaningful decisions for the future."

Relationships of Integrity Built on Trust. I described leadership first because it is central to the types of relationships that form within governance. Members of the governance group that reflected on their appreciation for the group process had developed a particular kind of relationship. They described their respect and mutual trust for one another. This enabled them to work together in ways that differed from the governance units they had previously been involved with. One member stated, "[Over the years], I have served on close to a hundred task forces, committees, the senate, and planning groups. This was the first time I have developed these types of relationships, and it changed the nature of our work as well as outcomes and policies developed. I feel that the work of this group had more integrity." Within the governance process, leaders are instrumental in setting a tone for the types of relationships that will develop.

But why are relationships critical to effective governance? The answer is that effective governance depends on people being willing to share their insights and ideas. Unless there are relationships of respect and trust, people do not share ideas. One member of a campus planning committee described his experience of mutual respect on a committee and how it altered the work of the committee: "Being trusted with information, being valued, and getting extensive communication have changed the nature of the dialogue; we are coming up with creative ideas that I have never seen before in my thirty years on the campus."

Relationships of integrity are crucial if people are to get outside of personal agendas and work together toward institutional policy setting. In effective governance people are able to examine evidence and data, getting beyond their personal biases and interests and focusing instead on the common good. Individuals in the case studies I conducted told how relationships nurtured in the governance process enabled them to develop quality decisions they could be proud of, as in this example: "There is a big difference between the groups that I have seen make strong decisions and those that make no or problematic decisions. From my experience, it comes down to the relationships among the people in the decision-making body. These relationships can be formed informally outside the governance context or within the governance group. So, it doesn't matter how or where they are formed, but good decisions generally require people who can work together well. And working well doesn't mean 'happy talk,' it means civil debate and respect."

When bonds among participants in the group are tightened, the group becomes better able to work as a team and to develop cognitively complex decisions and policy—that is, decisions that take into account more perspectives and evidence (for more details about teams and cognitive complexity, see Bensimon and Neumann, 1993). Relationships were also critical for decisions being seen as legitimate by members of the group and therefore by others on campus. All too often people leave a committee or senate meeting only to tell everyone about the disastrous decision or policy that was just made. When there are relationships of integrity among people, those people are less likely to speak disparagingly about a decision and more likely to describe the reasons and rationale behind it, prompting ownership among their colleagues at the university.

Relationships and trust are hard to separate; good relationships lead to trust, and trust develops good relationships. There are two relationships in particular in which trust is critical to effective governance: the relationship between faculty and administrators (often epitomized by the relationship between senate chair and president), and the relationship between the president and his or her board. If trust does not exist in these relationships, effective governance is unlikely. On some campuses studied, lack of trust between various faculty groups also thwarted governance.

I was best able to understand why trust was so significant by examining campuses where trust did not exist. Generally, people on such campuses acted out of fear or anger. They did not communicate openly or honestly, they withheld data and information, they lobbied for an interest rather than listening, and they were unable to see common goals. Without trust, people did not feel safe. One person described the way the need to feel safe related to good governance: "In the past, I felt I could not trust people. The administration seemed to be working against the faculty, we were perceived as the enemy almost. When voting on policy, I was always suspicious— what is their angle? I would vote against things that seemed to make sense, knowing that in some way, it must work against faculty. And they never listened to us, so policies that came up, I knew had limited faculty input or perhaps none."

In this case, fear and anger prevented decisions that favored the overall interests of the campus. But where trust existed, people could step outside their specific interests and think about the campus as a whole. One story from a president helps illustrate this point. She was trying to alter transfer requirements, making it easier for students to come in from another school. She worried that it would be a horrible struggle, but she knew the campus had been working to develop trust. To her surprise there was a willingness to change; no one came forth with the usual complaint that administration was just trying to increase numbers and didn't care whether students were smart or not. She noted how the faculty stayed centered on their values and mission by asking what was absolutely essential for a student to take in the curriculum to make them feel ready and at the same time not have as many hurdles to join us here. She was happy that faculty moved past old territorial patterns and more narrow concerns.

Conclusion

The evidence from the case studies I conducted is that leadership, trust, and relationships supersede structures and processes in effective decision making. A governance system can operate with imperfect structures and processes, but if leadership is missing and relationships and trust damaged, the governance system will likely fail for lack of direction, motivation, meaning, integrity, a sense of common purpose, ways to integrate multiple perspectives, open communication, people willing to listen, and legitimacy.

A new perspective is gaining support: campuses can build effective governance through an investment in leadership development and through mechanisms that nurture faculty, staff, and administrative relationships (for example, sponsoring campuswide events). These actions (fostering leadership development and building relationships) will also contribute positively to the intangibles of human interaction, such as trust. Investment in training for leaders is perhaps the best way to create better relationships and trust since leaders are pivotal in the development of both of these areas.

References

Association of Governing Boards of Universities and Colleges. *Renewing the Academic Presidency: Stronger Leadership for Tougher Times.* Washington, D.C.: Association of Governing Boards of Universities and Colleges, 1996.

Baldridge, J. *Power and Conflict in the University.* New York: Wiley, 1971.

Baldridge, J. "Shared Governance: A Fable About the Lost Magic Kingdom." *Academe,* Jan.–Feb. 1982, pp. 12–15.

Benjamin, R., and Carroll, S. "The Implications of the Changed Environment for Governance in Higher Education." In W. Tierney (ed.), *The Responsive University.* Baltimore: Johns Hopkins University Press, 1998.

Bensimon, E., and Neumann, A. Redesigning Collegiate Leadership. Baltimore: Johns Hopkins University Press, 1993.

Birnbaum, R. "The Cybernetic Institution: Toward an Integration of Governance Theories." *Higher Education,* 1989, *18,* 239–253.

Birnbaum, R. *How Colleges Work: The Cybernetics of Academic Organization and Leadership.* San Francisco: Jossey-Bass, 1991a.

Birnbaum, R. "The Latent Organizational Functions of the Academic Senate: Why Senates Do Not Work But Will Not Go Away." In M. W. Peterson, E. E. Chaffee, and T. H. White (eds.), *Organization and Academic Governance in Higher Education.* (4th ed.) Needham Heights, Mass.: Ginn Press, 1991b.

Birnbaum, R. *Management Fads in Higher Education.* San Francisco: Jossey-Bass, 2000.

Braskamp, L., and Wergin, J. "Forming New Social Partnerships." In W. Tierney (ed.), *The Responsive University: Restructuring for High Performance.* Baltimore: Johns Hopkins University Press, 1998.

Cohen M. D., and March, J. G. *Leadership and Ambiguity.* (2nd ed.) Boston: Harvard Business School Press, 1986.

Del Favero, M. "Faculty-Administrator Relationships as Integral to High Performing Governance Systems: New Frameworks for Study." *American Behavioral Scientist,* 2003, *46*(6), 901–922.

Dill, D. D., and Helm, K. P. "Faculty Participation in Policy Making." In J. Smart (ed.), *Higher Education: Handbook of Theory and Research.* New York: Agathon, 1988.

Dimond, J. "Faculty Participation in Institutional Budgeting." In R. Birnbaum (ed.), *Faculty in Governance: The Role of Senates and Joint Committees in Academic Decision Making.* New Directions for Higher Education, no. 75. San Francisco: Jossey-Bass, 1991.

Gilmour, J. E., Jr. "Participative Governance Bodies in Higher Education: Report of a National Study." In R. Birnbaum (ed.), *Faculty in Governance: The Role of Senates and Joint Committees in Academic Decision Making.* New Directions for Higher Education, no. 75. San Francisco: Jossey-Bass, 1991.

Kaplan, G. E. "Extending Public Choice Theory to Non-Governmental Democratic Structures of Decision: The Case of Higher Education." Unpublished paper, Graduate School of Public Affairs, University of Colorado, 2003.

Kezar, A., and Eckel, P. "Meeting Today's Governance Challenges: A Synthesis of the Literature and Examination of a Future Agenda for Scholarship." *Journal of Higher Education,* forthcoming.

Lee, B. "Campus Leaders and Campus Senates." In R. Birnbaum (ed.), *Faculty in Governance: The Role of Senates and Joint Committees in Academic Decision Making.* New Directions for Higher Education, no. 75. San Francisco: Jossey-Bass, 1991.

Massey, W. *Honoring the Trust: Quality and Cost Containment in Higher Education.* Bolton, Mass.: Anker, 2003.

Mintzberg, H. *The Professional Bureaucracy.* Upper Saddle River, N.J.: Prentice Hall, 1979.

Morgan, G. *Images of Organization.* Thousand Oaks, Calif.: Sage, 1997.

Mortimer, K., and McConnell, T. *Sharing Authority Effectively.* San Francisco: Jossey-Bass, 1979.

Schuster, J., Smith, D., Corak, K., and Yamada, M. *Strategic Academic Governance: How to Make Big Decisions Better.* Phoenix, Ariz.: Oryx Press, 1994.

Tierney, W. "Critical Leadership and Decision Making in a Postmodern World." In C. Brown (ed.), *Organization and Governance in Higher Education.* (5th ed.) Boston: Pearson Custom, 2000.

Weingartner, R. *Fitting Form to Function: A Primer on the Organization of Academic Organizations.* Phoenix, Ariz.: Oryx Press, 1996.

Wheatley, M. *Leadership and the New Science.* San Francisco: Berrett-Koehler, 1996.

Williams, D., Gore, W., Broches, C., and Lostski, C. "One Faculty's Perception of Its Academic Governance Role." *Journal of Higher Education,* 1987, *58,* 6.

ADRIANNA KEZAR is an associate professor with the University of Southern California's Higher Education Program. She is also editor of the ASHE-ERIC Higher Education Report series.

4

Twenty-first century conditions are adding new dimensions to the relationship between states and higher education.

The State and Higher Education: An Essential Partnership

Paul E. Lingenfelter

The relationship between higher education and the state has become essential, but it has never been easy. The precursors of the professors in modern colleges and universities are the ancient philosophers and scribes who passed along their knowledge and skills to apprentices. Their patrons and "governors" were undoubtedly private: the students and parents who supported them. Despite this beginning, however, the social importance of higher education has led inexorably to state involvement in virtually every nation.

In perhaps the first, most notorious state intervention, the democratic government of Athens condemned Socrates to death by suicide for corrupting the youth. Clearly, the people of Athens knew that they had a stake in higher education, even though it presumably was not tax supported. They sadly and foolishly expressed their fears and exercised their sovereignty by making Socrates a martyr.

In the martyrdom of Socrates, in the suppression of Galileo by the Catholic Church, and in far too many less famous cases, we find social and political leaders taking wrong-headed, tragic actions against scholars and intellectuals. Paradoxically, such events are both a warning about the abuse of state power and incontrovertible evidence that higher learning really matters. Fortunately, states have more often acted constructively, creating thousands of institutions and supporting millions of scholars charged with advancing and promulgating knowledge and preparing successive generations of professionals and social leaders.

Both history and contemporary practice affirm the deep interdependence between higher education and the state. The complexity and difficulty

NEW DIRECTIONS FOR HIGHER EDUCATION, no. 127, Fall 2004 © Wiley Periodicals, Inc.

of the relationship, however, is illustrated by an extensive literature. Richard Novak has catalogued more than one hundred books, reports, and major studies written on the topic in the United States alone from 1920 to 1995 (Novak, 1995).

Only the unread would aspire to make a wholly fresh contribution to this literature, but society's needs for higher education are changing in important ways. It is time to revisit fundamental issues and consider the implications of changing conditions.

Toward that end, this chapter will address three questions:

- What are the contemporary public purposes of higher education? How are they changing?
- What values should govern the relationship between higher education and the state?
- How can states deal with the practical issues of pursuing the public interest in higher education?

The Evolving Purposes of Higher Education

The first colleges of the United States were established with help from the colonies to preserve the community's religious and cultural heritage and to educate leaders for the ministry and the professions. After the Revolution the fledgling states began a long history of directly supporting colleges and universities, including helping now "private" colleges such as Harvard, Yale, and University of Pennsylvania over financial rocky spots (Rudolph, 1990). The public purposes of higher education evolved further as the people of the United States took the following series of policy actions:

- Created publicly owned "flagship universities" in each state
- Enacted the Morrill Act, signed by Abraham Lincoln, which created land grant colleges and universities to foster higher education in agriculture and engineering
- Developed universities and normal schools during the nineteenth century to train primary and secondary teachers and expand access to higher education
- Created and financed the GI Bill after World War II, for the first time enabling large numbers of lower- and middle-income people to obtain a higher education
- Created federally funded research programs to address human needs and promote the national interest
- Massively expanded public universities and created community college systems in the 1960s to educate the baby boom generation and to extend further the scope and reach of higher education
- Established federal and state student assistance programs to provide widespread access to higher education and greater choice among institutions

All of these actions were justified as essentially public, not private purposes. These initiatives implicitly argued that all people, whether or not they participate personally, benefit from and depend on the quality of higher education. While higher education clearly conveys broad social benefits, it is no longer an elite enterprise.

Some postsecondary education is now required for most jobs that support a middle-class lifestyle. More than 60 percent of high school graduates now enroll immediately in college the fall after graduating from high school, and virtually all young people in American high schools plan to attend postsecondary education.

Higher education is now expected not just to educate leaders, but also to provide economic opportunity for the masses and the large supply of skilled workers needed to assure general prosperity. In addition to workforce competence, the increasingly complex challenges of citizenship require advanced education for the general population. This is not a new idea. Ortega y Gassett (1966) persuasively and passionately made the case in his essay, *Mission of the University*, first published in 1944. The emergence of an economic order based increasingly on knowledge and skills has simply given it greater traction.

Now the public worries whether all able students can afford to attend a college or university, whether larger numbers of them are successfully completing rigorous academic programs, whether talented students are staying near home to attend college, whether they stay in the state to work, and whether the state's research university is attracting external grants and making discoveries that will help state businesses compete more successfully.

This change has profound implications for both states and colleges and universities. In the mid-twentieth century, higher education was considered appropriate for those who are most clever in school and who work hard at their studies, perhaps one-quarter or even one-third of the population. The path to excellence for institutions was to raise standards as high as possible, hire the best faculty, and enroll the smartest students.

In the twenty-first century, many more students are expected to succeed in postsecondary education. Perhaps another third, the middle third in the natural distribution of academic talent, is expected to attain a baccalaureate degree with no compromise on quality. Institutions are being asked to bear a substantial responsibility for their success.

Universities and colleges still pursue excellence through selectivity and the competition for resources. But civic leaders and policymakers are increasingly looking for ways of assessing the value institutions add to students, and they are working to hold institutions accountable for retention and degree completion.

This change of direction implicitly poses fundamental questions about human educability and the capacity of educators to facilitate higher achievement. Obviously, twenty-first century expectations place a heavier burden on both teachers and students, but educators will find the heavier burden less familiar.

What Purposes and Values Govern the Relationship Between Higher Education and the State?

The important freedoms of thought and expression, and the corollary freedoms to teach and to learn, often are the starting point for discussions of the relationship between higher education and the state. These basic human rights are essential to a good society and central to the public purposes of higher education. But freedom of inquiry and expression are not the whole purpose: they are part of a broader array of goals, principles, and values that shape the relationship between higher education and the state.

The fundamental value governing this relationship is the obligation of higher education to serve the public interest, broadly understood. The presumption of public service is the justification for the tax exemptions enjoyed by all nonprofit colleges and universities as well as the more direct governmental subsidies provided through student assistance, grants, contracts, and direct appropriations.

The public interest is a slippery concept, of course, which is why democratic societies elect representatives to debate and determine how it should be defined and pursued. While the details and even core principles may be contested, contemporary colleges and universities generally are expected to carry out the following functions:

- Transmit the knowledge and dispositions required for responsible citizenship and the perpetuation of the cultural heritage
- Teach the knowledge and skills required for productive employment in the professions and the workplace, increasingly for most of the adult population
- Expand knowledge continuously and facilitate its use to improve human life and the economic vitality of particular communities
- Provide an open forum for social criticism, free debate, and inquiry, and ensure that students learn how to participate in such conversations constructively
- Supply a means for achieving equality of opportunity and social mobility based on talent and effort, regardless of wealth, social position, or heritage
- Perform these functions effectively and efficiently, so that students learn successfully, useful knowledge expands, and the costs to society and the student are affordable.

Practical Challenges of Pursuing the Public Interest in Higher Education

Traditionally (with Socrates, Galileo, and more recent examples firmly in mind), the academy asserts that the core of its public purpose lies in its autonomy, the freedom of faculty to decide what to study, what to teach, and what to say about science, art, and society. Institutions of higher education are not only stubbornly independent about these things; they also require a good deal of money. These two characteristics pose large problems in developing state policy for higher education.

How can states reconcile the tension between the traditionally decentralized, independent, competitive character of the higher education industry and the need for accountability to a coherent public agenda? How can the states finance a system of higher education that is headed toward serving most of the population? How might such a system be different from or similar to traditional approaches to higher learning? States and educators need to think deeply about the fundamental issues at stake, the essential elements of excellent higher education, and what is required to achieve the public interest.

Autonomy and Freedom. At first glance, the idea of institutional autonomy seems entirely at odds with the equally compelling idea of accountability to a public agenda for higher education. If rightly understood, however, these ideas are not incompatible. All organizations have unavoidable responsibilities and dependencies; hence, absolute autonomy is impossible. The public interest requires that colleges and universities both enjoy important freedoms and bear significant public responsibilities.

Students and faculty must enjoy the freedom to teach, learn, and do research because these freedoms are fundamental to an open society and to human progress. Institutions, and especially public colleges and universities, have an obligation to nurture and sustain an environment where free inquiry and expression are encouraged and different ideas can be heard and debated.

This obligation does not require or even suggest that every viewpoint must have equal weight or be officially represented in the academy. Some ideas acquire a larger share in the marketplace of ideas, just as some goods and services acquire a larger market share in economic markets. But intellectual freedom requires openness to divergent perspectives, a robust exploration of such differences in responsible scholarship and teaching, and an active scholarly dialogue that permits and generates changes in prevailing thought.

From time to time some have accused colleges and universities of restricting freedom of expression because of a bias in favor of or against particular points of view. Academic leaders have a responsibility to take such charges seriously, to investigate them, and to address them if supported by evidence. History suggests, however, that serious challenges to intellectual freedom tend to come from the exercise of state power far more than from "group think" in the academy. When the power of the state is interjected into the intellectual life of any community, especially an academic community, the public interest in freedom of thought is at risk.

Pursuing the public interest in the operational details of colleges and universities, a different matter, requires balancing freedom and accountability along a number of practical dimensions. Institutions must be accountable for using public resources responsibly, for addressing public priorities, and for pursuing their missions effectively. The state has a right and responsibility to allocate resources to public priorities and to hold institutions accountable for achieving them.

The key test for state intervention on operational matters is the same as the test that should keep the state out of intellectual content: What is in the public interest? The state should be legitimately concerned about whether the programmatic offerings of colleges and universities meet student demand and the needs of employers and society; whether institutional costs and prices are appropriate; and whether program quality is acceptable.

While the public interest must be asserted in such fundamental matters, wise states leave most operational details to institutional administrators and governing boards. Educators need flexibility and agility to be efficient and to meet changing public needs. "The Efficiency of Freedom," the 1959 report of the national Committee on Government and Higher Education, chaired by Milton Eisenhower, cited numerous examples of costly and ineffective purchasing and hiring regulations imposed on colleges and universities. Some of these still exist. States need to judge wisely both the questions for which institutions should be held accountable and the means for doing so.

Money and Accountability. Because its objective is the expansion of knowledge and learning in the human race, the aspirations and appetite of higher education for resources legitimately, but unrealistically, have no upper limit. Bowen (1977) was surely not the first to recognize this, but he made the point famously. The insatiable appetite of colleges and universities for money and their (mostly salutary) drive to compete with each other enormously complicate the job of developing public policies for higher education. Quality, access, and cost control cannot simultaneously be maximized. In fact, in higher education, quality and widespread participation are deeply in conflict with cost control.

Institutional competition to enhance quality and attract students tends to push up the cost of higher education. While parents and students surely must prefer lower prices, to a point anyway, they apparently do not prefer them at the expense of access and quality. Student enrollments have continued to grow even as prices have increased, and institutions have tended to compete more on quality than on price.

To the extent that high-quality higher education is high priced, generous support for student financial aid is needed to provide access and opportunity to low- and middle-income students. When states have tried to keep public tuitions lower, increasingly larger direct subsidies have been needed to maintain competitive quality.

Without substantial public subsidies for institutional support or student assistance, widespread, successful participation and excellent quality are not feasible. Without resources and freedom to compete in the complex market of higher education, institutions are unlikely to achieve and sustain excellence. Without mechanisms to sort through these issues and allocate public subsidies intelligently, it becomes impossible to achieve an acceptable level of cost-effectiveness.

One approach to this dilemma would be simply to let the marketplace determine all prices for higher education by limiting public support to student aid and ending direct support of institutions of higher education. This idea's simplicity and reliance on customer choice have appeal. Almost certainly, however, the highest-quality, most prestigious educational experiences would have, by far, the highest prices. Moreover, educational opportunity for low- and moderate-income students would depend entirely on the adequacy, reliability, and effectiveness of student financial aid programs. It is easy to imagine what would be at risk in hard economic times.

Alternatively, governments could increase public regulation and diminish the extent to which institutions of higher education are competitive—making higher education a public monopoly or a much more heavily regulated public utility. This could control costs without diminishing participation and equity of access, but it would likely lead to an unacceptable deterioration of quality and a reduction in the private resources now donated to institutions.

The states and the nation have taken a middle path—typically, providing direct institutional subsidies to public institutions, along with relative operational autonomy and relatively modest tuition rates. In many states students attending private institutions are supported through state student aid and, in some cases, direct institutional grants.

Although the states have consistently chosen the middle path, it is not an easy road to travel. It requires them constantly to manage, to fine-tune, and to balance, rather than to resolve the legitimate values in conflict. High stakes and the complexity of these issues demand sustained, thoughtful attention to the development and implementation of policy affecting higher education. A related conflict involves the private and public benefits that accrue from successful completion of higher education. In effect, policies determining public tuitions and direct public subsidies for institutions reflect a judgment about the appropriate balance between these values.

States also have taken a mixed approach to institutional autonomy for public institutions. On one hand, lay boards govern and coordinate public institutions, creating a degree of autonomy. On the other hand, states regulate the operations of public institutions, sometimes substantially, and they have implemented procedures to assure accountability to public purposes. States have also imposed regulations and requirements on private institutions as a condition of receiving public support and as a means of consumer protection.

Neither the desire of higher education for resources nor the desire of governmental leaders for accountability and cost-effectiveness can be easily or permanently satisfied. Achieving the public interest in higher education requires things that are fundamentally in conflict: institutions with enough freedom to be responsive, competitive, effective, and efficient; responsiveness to public needs as articulated by democratically elected representatives; a substantial commitment of public resources to achieve quality and access; and cost-effectiveness. No matter how broad-minded, sympathetic, and well meaning, governmental officials and higher education leaders will have different perspectives on these issues.

Shaping Higher Education Policy

Good institutional governance is critically important to a good state system of higher education, but it is not sufficient. Every state also needs an effective means of articulating and pursuing the public agenda for higher education. That work, as suggested above, is a constant balancing act between legitimate but conflicting values.

The Job Description. Conceived broadly, the work includes six tasks:

1. Collecting and providing public access to comprehensive, relevant data on higher education to help the state develop its vision and agenda for higher education.
2. Analyzing and articulating policy issues—workforce needs, pK–12 student preparation, student aspirations and demand, research needs and opportunities, the affordability of higher education to students and their families, and the needs of different geographical regions.
3. Understanding deeply the contributions, potential, and limitations of existing resources (institutional and otherwise) to meet these needs.
4. Working with educators to develop and implement strategies to meet state needs and to increase higher education's quality, efficiency, and productivity.
5. Working with the governor and legislature to develop and gain support for an agenda for higher education that addresses their priorities and vision for the state.
6. Helping the governor and legislature develop budget allocations that address state priorities, reflect the state's fiscal capacities, address the needs and utilize the resources of existing institutions and programs, and enhance the cost-effectiveness of higher education.

These tasks can be done in a variety of ways and in a variety of structures. But effective state policy requires that all of them be done well.

Doing the Job. States have approached this problem in different ways. Among the states there are statewide governing or coordinating boards for higher education, a few state boards with oversight and policy responsibilities for all levels of public education, and one state without a statewide board for higher education.

Why haven't the states come up with a uniform approach? Possibly because *they* are different, possibly because every generation seems compelled to question and tinker with governance questions, and possibly because different approaches seem to work reasonably well. In that light, is a state's coordination and governance scheme for higher education irrelevant?

No. But surprisingly, it is not whether a state has a governing or coordinating board that seems to make a difference. What seems to matter is whether the state uses whatever structure it has to deal effectively with the fundamental problems of state policy. What does it take to do this job well?

Although other issues are relevant, these four are especially important: the need for clearly assigning responsibility for policy regarding state higher education; the importance of a lay board in establishing continuity and public consensus; accountability to elected officials; and the alignment and coordination of pK–12 and higher education.

Somebody's Job. The "job description" for shaping higher education policy must be assigned to somebody as a professional responsibility. Conceivably, this assignment could be given to a legislative staff group, an executive agency, the staff of a statewide governing board, or the staff of a statewide coordinating board. Regardless of who does the work, somebody needs to be held accountable for the expertise and the sustained attention required to do the job well.

It is important to stress that the job described here includes responsibility for neither legislation nor institutional operations. Those jobs belong to elected representatives, to institutional administrators, and to faculty. The distinctive professional role outlined here is to stand as a facilitator between ultimate policymaking authority and institutional operations. Those performing this role stand in the service of both those who have formal authority for developing policy and those who have responsibility for implementing it, much like a broker serving two clients.

Unfortunately, in many states public policy for higher education has not received the explicit, sustained attention that it requires. Such policy is too important and too complicated to be ignored or assigned as an occasional, part-time duty of people who have many other responsibilities. If a state decides to vest this responsibility in a legislative staff or an executive agency, the people involved should be assigned full time to this area, not also assigned to other functions of government. Moreover, they should have the breadth of expertise and credibility needed to work effectively with all the governmental and educational constituencies involved.

The same principle holds if the responsibility is vested in the staff of a statewide governing board for institutions of higher education. If a statewide governing board is responsible for advising the governor and legislature on broad-scale public policy for higher education, the board must do more than govern public institutions. It must devote some of its staff resources and board time explicitly and deeply to these public policy issues. Simply doing a good job of institutional governance is insufficient.

Among the models commonly employed, only statewide coordinating boards for higher education focus solely on policy, undiluted by institutional governance or distracted by the comprehensive responsibilities of elected officials. The coordinating board's focus on policy can be a wasted resource, however, if elected officials and institutional leaders do not work with the board to develop an ongoing policy consensus. Both state government and higher education have a stake in a strong, credible brokering relationship.

The Importance of a Lay Board

Although the job of focusing on higher education policy could be assigned to an executive or legislative agency, experience suggests that things work better when it is assigned to a lay board that reports to both the governor and legislature.

Education is not a branch of government, but virtually every state has established governing or coordinating boards to provide some measure of separation between government and the operation of schools, colleges, and universities. These boards are only occasionally granted full constitutional autonomy, but their independent status serves clear purposes. One is to provide a vehicle for the involvement of the private sector in public policy affecting higher education. Another is to provide a degree of professional autonomy to educators, helping to insulate them from short-term pressures of the partisan political process. Such professional autonomy is limited and conditional; it is granted *because* it is essential for building institutions that, over the long haul, will serve the public interest.

Lay boards should have responsibility for submitting recommendations on public policy to elected officials who, for most policy issues, will have ultimate authority. Lay boards are more likely to provide the stability of leadership and continuity needed to build a long-term perspective for higher education policy.

The staff of a lay board is also likely to be more capable of doing the most challenging aspect of the job description—working effectively with all the political and educational constituencies that have a stake in public policy affecting higher education. A legislative staff or the governor's staff is much more likely to become entangled in issues unrelated to higher education or in partisan political matters.

Obviously, these advantages of a lay board do not endow them with ultimate wisdom. Lay boards and their staff can be ineffective if they do not establish working relationships with elected officials; they must be held accountable for the public interest in higher education and for working effectively with both elected representatives and educational leaders.

States have developed various approaches to assure that lay board members are broadly representative and that they have a fair chance of building consensus across partisan party lines. A working, bipartisan consensus on education has become more difficult as political leaders compete for leadership in reform, but it is no less necessary. A state system of higher education cannot thrive if it is a significant factor in partisan conflict or if its leaders depend on political patronage.

Accountability to Elected Officials

The elected representatives of the people have the last word in public policy for higher education just as they do for every other matter of law and public policy in a democracy. It is not possible to develop and implement public policy effectively without their cooperation, involvement, leadership, and consent. The principle of being insulated from the political process goes too far if it also means that policy for higher education is insulated from the passions and priorities of the governor and legislature.

Within the time-honored tradition of checks and balances built into state and federal constitutions, a variety of workable approaches have been developed to hold higher education accountable without direct political control. Of course, any approach, including those discussed favorably below, can work badly if those involved violate the spirit of shared power and cooperative action.

A system in which governors have the power to appoint members of lay boards to fixed terms of office, staggered so that the boards have continuity over any governor's single term, provides both political responsiveness and stability. For statewide policy responsibilities, it is also helpful if the chair of a lay board serves at the pleasure of the governor. This practice is likely to assure that the governor has a strong voice, but not the only voice in shaping the deliberations of a state board charged with developing policy recommendations for higher education. It also is likely to ensure that the views of the statewide board will have a fair hearing in the executive branch.

In some states the governor plays an even stronger role, appointing the chief executive of the statewide board for higher education or having that person, appointed by a lay board, sit as a member of the governor's cabinet. If the governor does not appoint the chair of the board, having the executive director or chancellor serve in the cabinet can achieve some of those purposes.

The ability of a statewide board to work effectively with legislative and institutional constituencies is stronger if its chief executive is not a formally appointed member of the governor's cabinet. A statewide policy board obviously must work closely with the governor in order to be effective, but it can be helpful, even to the governor, for the board also to have a credible, independent role with the legislature and institutions.

A statewide board should have a clear responsibility to articulate and pursue the public interest and a public agenda for higher education, working with political leaders, but not as part of the partisan political process.

In specific situations, both institutions and elected officials will want the board to be unambiguously on their side. Elected officials will want a compliant board when things are tough; institutions will want the board to be a strong advocate for their needs and wants.

An effective board must be perceived as partially on everybody's side, but wholly on the side of the best possible higher education policy for the state. This means that the board will challenge elected officials to do their very best on behalf of the public interest in higher education, and it will challenge institutions to do their very best on behalf of the public. Elected officials and institutional leaders will not always welcome such challenges, but they will benefit from them if they are based on expertise, good information, and sensitivity to both sides.

While it is rarely easy, a statewide board can obtain support from both elected officials and institutions. First, the foundation of its credibility should be its leadership and that of its staff in articulating and pursuing the public agenda for higher education. It then must demonstrate a willingness to listen carefully to all perspectives, work for mutual understanding, respond promptly and professionally to the requests of elected officials, and, at the end of the day, implement the decisions of duly elected public officials whether or not they reflect perfectly the board's own views.

Conclusion

State policymaking for higher education is at a critical juncture. In the late 1950s and early 1960s Sputnik inspired far-reaching educational reforms and the states mobilized to educate the baby boom generation. Today the core issue is assuring that the next generation, which will be competing in the global, knowledge economy, has a fair shot at economic opportunity and prosperity.

Policy for higher education has never been easy for the states. The mixture of private and public benefits involved; the decentralized, competitive nature of the industry; its unquenchable thirst for resources; and the tradition of professional and institutional autonomy pose difficult challenges for the political process.

But sustained financial support and good state policy are essential. The public interest requires states to get on top of policy issues affecting higher education. They must find a path leading to the public's goal—high quality, affordable cost, and widespread, successful participation. That path must include balancing the legitimate values that compete for priority and protecting the attributes of higher education that are the foundation of its quality and contributions to society.

References

Bowen, H. R. *Investment in Learning: The Individual and Social Value of American Higher Education.* San Francisco: Jossey-Bass, 1977.

Committee on Government and Higher Education. *The Efficiency of Freedom.* Washington, D.C.: American Association of State Colleges and Universities, 1985. (Originally published 1959.)

Novak, R. *Statewide Governance, Coordination, and Trusteeship in Public Higher Education: An Annotated Bibliography.* Washington, D.C.: Association of Governing Boards of Universities and Colleges, 1995.

Ortega y Gasset, J. *Mission of the University.* New York: Norton, 1966.

Rudolph, F. *The American College and University: A History.* Athens, Ga.: University of Georgia Press, 1990.

PAUL E. LINGENFELTER is executive director of SHEEO, the national association of State Higher Education Executive Officers.

5

Research centers and institutes are one example of how institutional governance has become increasingly disjointed; as the "suburbs" of the university expand, core governance structures lose influence.

Disjointed Governance in University Centers and Institutes

William Mallon

The American research university, like the modern metropolis, is sprawling, and the most significant growth is occurring in the suburbs, not the center. Activities such as for-profit curricular ventures, strategic research alliances, distance education, and technology transfer testify to the increasingly far-flung enterprise of higher education. In these congested suburbs of the university, new models of decision making have emerged. Consequently, this is where scholars need to focus investigations of academic governance. Some have already begun to do so. Kennedy (1993), for instance, argued for "new coalitions" of decision makers from both the institutional center and its periphery (p. 113). Bok (2003) called for new decision-making models for entrepreneurial ventures. Kezar and Eckel (forthcoming) considered how new kinds of academic workers make "shared" governance more complex and problematic.

I want to explore conceptually what others have done anecdotally. Asserting that university governance is disjointed, I argue that certain structures, processes, and participants—in what I am calling the suburbs of the institution—have captured a role in decision making, infringing on how traditional governance works. I will examine the case of research centers and institutes in order to demonstrate how this disjointedness adds to and complicates traditional governance in the research university.

The author would like to thank Ann Austin, Peter Eckel, Bill Tierney, and members of the 2003 National Research Forum on Governance for their constructive readings of earlier drafts of this chapter.

A Framework of Disjointed Governance

Several scholars have used the term *disjointed* to call attention to the fragmented nature of institutional processes and individual actions. In their analysis of how researchers make decisions, Braybrooke and Lindblom (1963) argued that policy analysis and evaluation are disjointed because analysts investigate problems at a certain point only, without consideration of the whole issue and without an articulation of the various parts. They also argued that policy recommendations tend to be those that happen to be at hand rather than those that are chosen through comprehensive analysis of alternatives. For Braybrooke and Lindblom, then, "disjointed" describes a thought process in which there is no articulation of the various parts of the whole, no consideration of the interaction among parts, and a lack of comprehensive strategy to meet a set of goals.

Schickler (2001) borrowed the "disjointed" qualifier to describe organizational change. His analysis of Congress described the way that institutional change is layered over time, with each reform sought by a different coalition promoting a different interest. His theory of disjointed pluralism portrayed institutions "as multilayered historical composites that militate against any overarching order. . . . Congressional development is disjointed in that members incrementally add new institutional mechanisms, without dismantling preexisting institutions and without rationalizing the structure as a whole" (pp. 17–18).

Applying these theories to higher education, institutional governance can be best understood not as an overarching concept but as an aggregation of disjointed structures, processes, and employment patterns. Institutions of higher education, especially large research universities, have created different avenues of governance that, to paraphrase Schickler (2001), have produced a tense layering of new forms on old. Institutions have added these new governance mechanisms incrementally, without dismantling preexisting structures—even if those original forms are ineffective (Birnbaum, 1991).

Disjointed governance in universities is not dissimilar to the interaction among regional governments in a large metropolitan area. While the city council may have the most power and influence over the city center (where, historically, most business and commerce has been situated), important policy decisions that influence the whole metropolis are being made in the outlying suburbs, without alignment to any cohesive citywide plan. In the university, disjointed governance means that "suburban" decision making can adapt quickly at the periphery without engaging core decision makers. But just as decisions made in suburban communities can have profound consequences for the city center (for example, the creation of a research and technology park to attract new business), so, too, can adaptive decision-making structures change the core of the university. The expansion of the boundaries of the university has been furtive, but it has had a nonetheless significant impact on how universities operate.

Examples of Disjointed Decision Making

University governance has become increasingly disjointed over time. First, universities have introduced an abundance of new governance structures. Scholars have focused attention on many of these, including strategic-planning groups (Schuster, Smith, Corak, and Yamada, 1994), specialized committees (Yamada, 1991), and task forces (Hartley, 2003). The result has been a complex maze of governance, where participants' responsibilities and authority are increasingly confusing and uncertain.

Second, university governance has become more disjointed because there are now more decision makers. Historically, academic decision making has been shared among trustees, administrations, and faculty. As universities have become more commercialized (Bok, 2003), external constituencies—governors and legislatures, donors, for-profit competitors, strategic partners, and the federal government—have played an increasing role in how universities make decisions. As Chait (2002) noted, "changes in market conditions have reduced the influence of faculty, administrators, and, to a somewhat lesser degree, lay boards, and augmented the sway of external constituencies" (p. 315).

Power and influence within the faculty have also become more dispersed. Historically, faculty participation in governance was oligarchic (Clark, 1968): tenured faculty made the most important decisions (who gets hired, who gets tenure) and were joined by tenure-track professors for other decisions (what gets taught, when it gets taught). But these traditional appointment types no longer represent the majority of faculty. By the late 1990s, nontraditional faculty (part-timers, non-tenure-track faculty) made up more than 50 percent of all faculty appointments at research and doctoral universities (Anderson, 2002). By 1999, 55 percent of all new full-time faculty were hired into non-tenure-eligible term or contract appointments (Finkelstein and Schuster, 2001). Added to this mix are other faculty-like groups, such as postdoctoral appointees, non-faculty researchers, and graduate and research assistants.

With the increased diversity of faculty types on campuses, notions of academic citizenship have become more pluralistic. These new coalitions of faculty and instructional staff have begun to demand and win a role in the operational and decision-making structure in university affairs. Part-time and non-tenure-track faculty at several universities, for example, have their own faculty senates (Chait, 2002). Baldwin and Chronister (2001) found that in a sample of eighty-six four-year institutions, 84 percent of full-time, non-tenure-track faculty could participate in department committees, and 50 percent were eligible for the faculty senate. Some universities have also extended privileges previously reserved for tenured or tenure-track faculty to contract faculty. Stanford University, for instance, now permits non-tenure-track faculty to be principal investigators on extramurally supported grants (Ritcher, 2003).

As these examples demonstrate, nontraditional faculty and other faculty-like groups—which now compose a large majority of academic staff—participate in governance via both traditional pathways and alternative structures. Core faculty increasingly have to compete with these groups. The disjointed nature of participants in governance begs the question of whether we can even talk about "the faculty" as a monolith. When considering issues of power, influence, and participation, there is not one collective interest of faculty, but many *faculties*.

Similarly, there is more than one governance paradigm at the university. While shared governance among three traditional groups (faculty, administrators, trustees) may be a useful concept in some aspects of university life, ultimately it only describes a circumscribed, and shrinking, core of responsibilities. Other organization and governance structures exist in the suburbs of the university, and their importance is growing. Together, research centers and institutes form but one of the layers in this fragmented metropolis.

The Case of Research Centers and Institutes

The disjointed nature of governance in the research university is particularly apparent in one arena: organized research units. I use "centers" and "institutes" interchangeably to talk about these non-departmental organizational units that have a primary mission of research. I am not interested in service facilities such as libraries, computer laboratories, and instrumentation facilities that offer support services for researchers.

Many different types of centers exist. Ikenberry and Friedman (1972) categorized centers as standard, adaptive, or shadow. *Standard* centers are permanent bureaucracies with stable goals, finances, and personnel. *Adaptive* centers have minimal permanent staff and limited resources, and they constantly redefine their goals. *Shadow* units are those that primarily exist in the center director's file cabinet, with little outside funding, no staff, and no physical space. Centers can be department based, interdisciplinary, or even interinstitutional. For this discussion, I am primarily interested in interdisciplinary standard and adaptive centers, not department-based or shadow centers.

Research centers and institutes have always occupied a controversial place in higher education in the United States. Some observers excoriate their form as marginal to the mission of the university. The great higher education reformer Abraham Flexner was perhaps the earliest critic of these organizational add-ons. In 1930 he wrote that centers "may mean something or nothing" and derided Harvard's Institute of Criminal Law as "simply the name for the research activities of the chair devoted to that subject—a dubious departure, since it implies a possible separation of teaching and research with the limits of a university chair" (p. 111). Proponents counter that by focusing on particular research activities and being responsive to societal needs and interests, centers and institutes have contributed to the ascendancy of the great U.S. research university (Geiger, 1990).

Despite the debate, the research center and institute model has blossomed. According to the *Research Center Directory,* a biennial compendium of such entities, U.S. universities had created six thousand centers by 1980, ten thousand by 1990, and more than thirteen thousand by 2003 (Hedblad, 2003). Actually, these figures are surely undercounts because of the directory's collection methods. It would be difficult for observers of higher education to notice the growth of these organizational entities and not wonder about their rightful role.

Such ruminations are especially important in certain fields, such as the biomedical sciences, where research advances have affected organizational forms. In the biomedical sciences, the most promising avenues of research transcend disciplinary boundaries (Blue Ridge Academic Health Group, 2001; Ludmerer, 1999). In response to the progress of biomedical science and technology, many institutions have closed, consolidated, or merged departments (Mallon, Biebuyck, and Jones, 2003). In other cases, interdisciplinary research centers and institutes have proliferated (Rubin and Lindeman, 2001). Some of the nation's largest and most prestigious universities have created interdisciplinary centers to capitalize on the nexus of scientific advancement, economic development, and government and private funding. Here are some examples:

The Carolina Center for Genome Sciences at University of North Carolina–Chapel Hill involves faculty specializing in cancer epidemiology, cardiovascular disease, medical and bioinformatics, and statistical genetics. These faculty members are drawn from the College of Arts and Sciences, the School of Information and Library Sciences, and five health science schools: medicine, public health, pharmacy, dentistry, and nursing.

The University of Michigan Life Sciences Institute involves faculty from six schools; two dozen researchers will be housed in a $100 million, 230,000-square-foot facility.

The Institute for Bioengineering, Biotechnology, and Quantitative Biomedical Research at the University of California transcends not only disciplines but academic institutions as well. The Institute is a collaboration between three University of California campuses (Berkeley, San Francisco, and Santa Cruz), and is organized around three research modules—bioengineering and biotechnology, bioinformatics, and structural and chemical biology.

The existence of these entities testifies to the increasing importance of "big" biomedical science—as sources of institutional prestige and funding and as engines of economic development. Furthermore, evidence suggests that biomedical centers and institutes are moving from the margins toward the mainstream of the university. Some research centers serve as loci of primary appointment, offer tenured appointments, and influence institutional policymaking. These developments have led faculty and chairs to worry about a loss of departmental integrity, power, and funding (Fischman, 1998; Ibrahim and others, 2003).

The Role of Centers and Institutes in Academic Governance

The role of centers and institutes in academic governance is twofold. First, like departments, centers are loci for unit-level decision making by academic staff. Second, centers are involved in institution-level governance.

Unit-Level Governance. A discussion of center and institute governance must begin with a comparison to the academic department. The academic department developed in the 1890s with the rise of the modern research university. It was developed to take control over faculty appointment and tenure decisions, scheduling, and curriculum planning; that is, tasks that the university president could no longer handle alone (Geiger, 1986; Higham, 1979). Department chairs were, at first, quite authoritarian and dictatorial; as a counterbalance, in 1911, the University of Chicago began the trend of elected chairs (Hawkins, 1979). By the early 1900s, the department in U.S. universities took on a collegial decision-making culture (Clark and Youn, 1997). As a part of that culture, faculty typically elect the department chair or rotate the post among senior members (Hecht and others, 1999). Chairs have limited power over colleagues and cannot lead without faculty support (Hecht, Higgerson, Gmelch, and Tucker, 1999).

Centers and institutes, however, have a quite different governance model than departments (Friedman and Friedman, 1982; Ikenberry and Friedman, 1972; Rossi, 1964). A synthesis of the literature suggests that the typical shared governance model and collegial culture of the academic department do not extend to unit-level governance in the center. As shown in Table 5.1, differences are embodied in three aspects of unit-level governance: leadership, culture, and operating structure.

Unit leader. First, governance in centers differs from that in departments in the exercise of leadership. Academic departments are conceived as collegial bodies. The chair has limited positional authority. One cannot imagine, for instance, a chair instructing departmental faculty how to teach, what to teach, or on what to conduct research. The center director, however, rules with more power and control. This person has considerably more authority over how funding is allocated, who is hired and fired, and how the unit focuses its research effort, direction, and output. Center directors are likely to maintain their positional power. One study found that 69 percent of directors hold their offices indefinitely (Friedman and Friedman, 1982).

Operating culture. Centers also differ from departments in the culture of decision making. Departments typically embrace a culture of shared governance. The faculty, as a group, has the balance of power. In the center,

Table 5.1. Unit-Level Governance in the Center Versus the Department

Head of unit	Center Director	Department Chair
Length of appointment for head of unit	Typically indefinite or of undefined term. Those with a defined term typically can be renewed without limit	Typically elected by or rotating among senior-level faculty members in the department
Normative operating culture of unit	Authoritarian power of director	Consensus-driven or collegial model; shared among full-time faculty, especially senior members
Internal structure	Varies, but tends not to rely on participatory decision making	Faculty working groups and committees

participatory decision making is less common (Friedman and Friedman, 1986). A culture of shared governance is replaced by a culture of authority exercised through the entrepreneurial power of the leader (Stahler and Tash, 1994).

Internal committee structure. Finally, centers and departments can differ in their use of internal committees. The academic department, reflecting the governance norms of the university, addresses internal operational and policy concerns through permanent and ad-hoc committees of faculty peers. As an illustration of this system, consider how departments make hiring decisions. Typically, a faculty committee interviews candidates and makes recommendations, and the chair formally extends the offer. In contrast, the internal organization and structure of the center is more business-like and hierarchical (Hays, 1991). While some centers may encourage significant input, in others the center director makes unilateral decisions.

Centers and institutes embody a more managerial, leader-driven approach to internal governance than the shared, collegial governance found in departments. This dynamic suggests that, while the university core may operate within the norms of shared governance and collegiality, the units in the periphery may be more corporate and hierarchical in their approach. Disjointed governance helps explain how universities can at once be corporate and collegial—these parallel norms and cultures are layered disjointedly, one on top of another.

Institution-Level Governance. Previous research has demonstrated that, traditionally, centers and institutes have had little role in university-wide decision making. Ikenberry and Friedman (1972), Hays (1991), and Stahler and Tash (1994) all concluded that centers and institutes are not well integrated into university governance. Researchers at centers are not "real" faculty members, lacking traditional faculty prerogatives, such as tenure and eligibility to academic senates (Kruytbosch and Messinger, 1968; Teich, 1982). Scholars have asserted that centers and institutes are not major contributors to the academic mission and governance structure of the university (Friedman and Friedman, 1982; Stahler and Tash, 1994). But in the emerging entrepreneurial university of the twenty-first century, these views may be outdated. Centers and institutes may exercise more influence in university governance than has been previously acknowledged, for three reasons: faculty recruitment, revenue generation, and staffing.

First, centers are important in institutional governance because they can play a role in who is hired. Thirty years ago, Ikenberry and Friedman (1972) found that two-thirds of research centers could not initiate faculty appointments (meaning, of course, that one-third could). Some universities have recently changed policies to allow centers to initiate or have a voice in faculty appointments. Emory University, for example, permits its institutes to make primary faculty appointments in core areas. The policy of Ohio State University directs both the head of the "tenure-initiating unit" (that is, the department) and the center director to share responsibility for drafting offers of appointment, conduct annual and promotional reviews, and collaborate on reappointment decisions.

Second, centers exert influence because they generate revenue. While firm statistics are difficult to find, centers and institutes earn millions of dollars for universities every year. Not only are most of them financially self-supporting, but many generate additional revenue for the university. One can speculate that centers and institutes have a voice in governance—formally or informally—because, as the adage says, money talks.

Third, centers and institutes have become more important in university affairs because they employ significant numbers of personnel, most notably postdoctoral appointees and research scientists. As universities have expanded biomedical research over the last three decades, they have hired scores of these staffers. In 1975, only 9.6 percent of university-based biomedical Ph.D.s were postdoctoral appointees and only 6.3 percent were research associates and research scientists. By 1997, those percentages doubled, to 18.1 percent and 13.8 percent, respectively (National Research Council, 2000). Conventional wisdom suggests that centers and institutes employ a sizeable portion of these groups.

So, while scholars have suggested that centers are "at" the university but not "of" it (Ikenberry and Friedman, 1972), surely units that employ thousands of personnel and generate millions of dollars are "of" the university and have a role in how it operates. In the domains of unit-level and institution-level decision making, centers and institutes can introduce change in the university without having to confront traditional governance or engage in normal decision-making procedures (Hays, 1991). Centers and institutes are examples of academic governance that occurs in an invisible, parallel, and disjointed universe. The role of centers in academic governance is often invisible because they operate under the radar of the vast majority of faculty members and administrators. Because they are not incorporated within normative governance processes, centers and institutes influence decision making informally, through one-on-one negotiation, and outside traditional processes. For example, an entrepreneurial center director who successfully negotiates more space or better facilities because of large research funding may be able to circumvent the typical bureaucratic governance process for such decisions.

Center participation in governance is parallel to university-wide governance in that many processes are duplicative but isolated. For example, at many universities the decision-making process for appointments of nonfaculty doctoral research staff is very similar to that for faculty appointments; such staff must have comparable credentials. Yet that appointment process occurs in a separate, parallel universe, with its own distinct set of policies and participants.

Finally, the participation of centers and institutes in university governance is disjointed. Often there is no logical connection between centers and departments, research staff and traditional faculty, or center directors and other policy makers. As a result, the university has become an amalgamation of structures that are tensely layered, one upon the other, existing without coordination or integration. Tension may occur at many levels. There are different rules and norms about personnel, funding, and space allocation; different motives, goals, and expectations about mission; different decision makers and different cultures for how decision making should work.

Implications of Disjointed Governance

The disjointedness of centers and institutes in institutional governance has allowed the university to be flexible and adaptive in expanding its research enterprise, and therefore, responsive in meeting the demands and expectations of society. At the same time, the stability and focus of departments have ensured the university's commitment to its core ideals. To invoke an earlier metaphor, the disjointed nature of governance and organization has permitted the university to expand its suburbs at the same time it has maintained a vibrant city center. The current challenge for the academy, like that for many U.S. metropolitan areas, is one of balance: can we effectively encourage growth in new areas without succumbing to unfettered, unplanned, and destructive sprawl?

For some commentators, the answer, so far, is "no" (Bok, 2003). As universities continue to expand activities once considered peripheral, traditional governance structures will be left with a shrinking core of responsibilities and jurisdiction while these parallel structures will continue to grow in importance and influence. Figure 5.1 illustrates this phenomenon of the institution's growing periphery. While some endeavors, such as athletics and continuing education, have been lurking in the suburbs for some time, newer manifestations of this growth include a number of other activities:

Corporate alliances and partnerships. Universities have developed partnerships with corporations both in research and teaching activity. These partnerships meld two cultures—corporate and academic—that introduce new decision-making structures into the university.

Public-private research partnerships. Similarly, universities and research organizations have entered into agreements to develop structures of economic development and business incubation through research efforts. For example, the Minnesota Partnership for Biotechnology and Medical Genomics, announced in 2003, is a public-private venture between the University of Minnesota and the Mayo Clinic. One of the elements is a joint coordinating committee between the university and the clinic to set research priorities and implement collaborations (University of Minnesota, 2003).

For-profit divisions and spin-offs. Bleak (2003) found that some for-profit arms of universities were created and managed quite differently than the normative culture of academic decision making would dictate. Their governance represented a nontraditional, business-like model for academe.

Technology transfer. Often, faculty members are deeply involved with creating profitable products and markets with their research discoveries. But technology transfer processes also represent an added layer of decision making on traditional governance.

The university has created these adaptive units to stay in tune with its environment and to be more responsive to external pressures without having to change, or even engage, its core. But the core has been affected nonetheless. I suggest that the increasing disjointedness of decision making has five implications for university governance.

First, as universities continue to delve into areas such as joint ventures, research partnerships, and profit-making enterprises, the relative importance of formal faculty governing bodies will decline. The entrepreneurs who lead these activities will have little time for the pace of traditional governance. Peripheral projects will be more responsive to the external environment and less reliant on the advice and input of internal constituencies.

Second, the disjointed nature of governance suggests a further disaggregation of the collective interest of the faculty to various groups of academic professionals. Part-timers, non-tenure-track and contract faculty, research scientists, and other instructional types will continue to secure pathways to represent their interests in an increasingly pluralistic system of campus governance. Those perquisites once tightly held only by tenured faculty (for example, faculty senate participation, policy committees, principal investigator status) will continue to be extended to other members of the academic labor force.

Third, faculty influence will also devolve from the faculty as a group to faculty members as individuals. Those professors who bring in large amounts of revenue or capital through sizable grants, discoveries, patents,

Figure 5.1. Organizational and Governance Sprawl of the "Center" and "Suburbs" of the University, 1935, 1960, and 1999

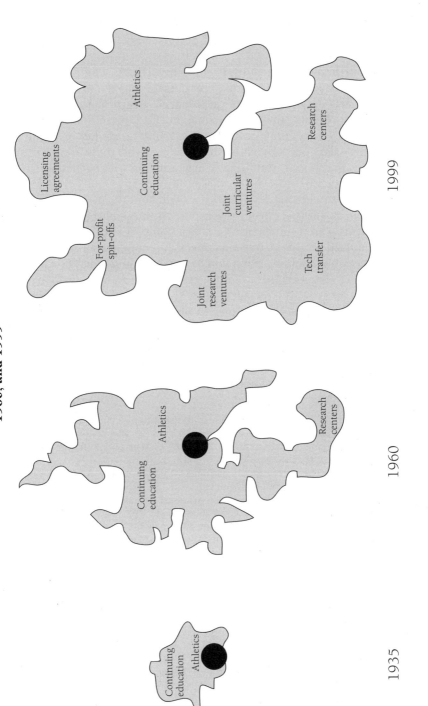

1999

1960

1935

or new technologies will find they have a voice in policymaking. As Chait (2002) summarized, "The power brokers are as likely, if not more likely, to be the professorial rain-makers and deal-makers than the faculty senate officers" (p. 312).

Fourth, as more faculty become involved in commercial activities, fewer will have the inclination to participate actively in formal channels of governance. As faculty hone their market instincts and secure external streams of revenue, they will become, in effect, entrepreneurial free agents with less loyalty to the institution. If a faculty researcher in a center covers all of her salary through extramural funding, what motivation will she have to serve on school committees, teach students, and participate in departmental activities?

Finally, centrifugal market forces will continue to push influence and power in governance from the center to the suburbs of the university. Modern research universities are vast complexes of commercial activity intermingled with academic missions. While commercial and programmatic activities once could be marginalized to the fringes—"at" the university but not "of" it—the periphery of alliances, ventures, and new enterprises will continue to grow. As a result there will be less influence at the center and less coordination at the margins. In turn, universities will need to embark on strategies for "smart growth" so that they do not become further disjointed and ultimately ungovernable.

References

Anderson, E. L. *The New Professoriate*. Washington, D.C.: American Council on Education, 2002.

Baldwin, R. G., and Chronister, J. L. *Teaching Without Tenure*. Baltimore, Md.: Johns Hopkins University Press, 2001.

Birnbaum, R. "The Latent Organizational Functions of the Academic Senate: Why Senates Do Not Work But Will Not Go Away." In M. W. Peterson, E. E. Chaffee, and T. W. White (eds.), *Organization and Academic Governance in Higher Education*. (4th ed.) Needham Heights, Mass.: Ginn Press, 1991.

Bleak, J. "Integrated or Insulated: The Governance of For-Profit Subsidiaries of Nonprofit Universities." Unpublished doctoral dissertation, Harvard University, 2003.

Blue Ridge Academic Health Group. *Creating a Value-Driven Culture in the Academic Health Center*. Charlottesville: University of Virginia, 2001.

Bok, D. *Universities in the Marketplace: The Commercialization of Higher Education*. Princeton, N.J.: Princeton University Press, 2003.

Braybrooke, D., and Lindblom, C. E. *A Strategy of Decision: Policy Evaluation as a Social Process*. New York: Free Press, 1963.

Chait, R. P. "The 'Academic Revolution' Revisited." In S. Brint (ed.), *The Future of the City of Intellect: The Changing American University*. Stanford, Calif.: Stanford University Press, 2002.

Clark, B. R. "The New University." In C. E. Kruytbosch and S. L. Messinger (eds.), *The State of the University: Authority and Change*. Thousand Oaks, Calif.: Sage, 1968.

Clark, B. R., and Youn, T.I.K. "The Historical Emergence of American Academic Organizations." In T.I.K. Youn, and P. B. Murphy (eds.), *Organizational Studies in Higher Education*. New York: Garland, 1997.

Finkelstein, M. J., and Schuster, J. H. "Assessing the Silent Revolution." *AAHE Bulletin,* Oct. 2001, pp. 3–7.

Fischman, D. A. "What Role Will Chairs of Discipline-Based Subjects Play in the Evolving Medical School of the Future?" *FASEB Journal,* 1998, *12,* 621–624.

Flexner, A. *Universities: American, English, German.* New York: Oxford University Press, 1930.

Friedman, R. S., and Friedman, R. C. "The Role of University-Organized Research Units in Academic Science." University Park: Pennsylvania State University Center for the Study of Higher Education, 1982.

Friedman, R. S., and Friedman, R. C. "Sponsorship, Organization, and Program Change at One Hundred Universities." University Park: Pennsylvania State University Institute for Policy Research and Evaluation, 1986.

Geiger, R. L. *To Advance Knowledge: The Growth of American Research Universities, 1900–1940.* New York: Oxford University Press, 1986.

Geiger, R. L. "Organized Research Units—Their Role in the Development of University Research." *Journal of Higher Education,* 1990, *61,* 1–19.

Hartley, M. "The Promise and Peril of Parallel Governance Structures." *American Behavioral Scientist,* 2003, *46*(7), 923–945.

Hawkins, H. "University Identity: The Teaching and Research Functions." In A. Olson, and J. Voss (eds.), *The Organization of Knowledge in Modern America.* Baltimore, Md.: Johns Hopkins University Press, 1979.

Hays, S. W. "From Adhocracy to Order: Organizational Design for Higher Education Research and Service." *Research Management Review,* 1991, *5*(2), 1–17.

Hecht, I. W., Higgerson, M. L., Gmelch, W. H., and Tucker, A. *The Department Chair as Academic Leader.* Phoenix, Ariz.: Oryx Press, 1999.

Hedblad, A. (ed.). *Research Centers Directory.* Detroit: Gale, 2003.

Higham, J. "The Matrix of Specialization." In A. Olson and J. Voss (eds.), *The Organization of Knowledge in Modern America.* Baltimore, Md.: Johns Hopkins University Press, 1979.

Ibrahim, T., and others. "Centers, Institutes, and the Future of Clinical Departments." *American Journal of Medicine,* 2003, *115,* 337–341.

Ikenberry, S. O., and Friedman, R. C. *Beyond Academic Departments.* San Francisco: Jossey-Bass, 1972.

Kennedy, D. "Making Choices in the Research University." In J. R. Cole, E. G. Barger, and S. R. Graubard (eds.), *The Research University in a Time of Discontent.* Baltimore, Md.: Johns Hopkins University Press, 1993.

Kezar, A., and Eckel, P. "Meeting Today's Governance Challenges: A Synthesis of the Literature and Examination of a Future Agenda for Scholarship." *Journal of Higher Education,* forthcoming.

Kruytbosch, C. E., and Messinger, S. L. "Unequal Peers: The Situation of Researchers at Berkeley." *American Behavioral Scientist,* May-June 1968, pp. 33–42.

Ludmerer, K. M. *Time to Heal: American Medical Education from the Turn of the Century to the Era of Managed Care.* New York: Oxford University Press, 1999.

Mallon, W. T., Biebuyck, J. F., and Jones, R. F. "The Reorganization of Basic Science Departments in U.S. Medical Schools, 1980–1999." *Academic Medicine,* 2003, *78,* 302–306.

National Research Council. *Addressing the Nation's Changing Needs for Biomedical and Behavioral Scientists.* Washington, D.C.: National Academy Press, 2000.

Ritcher, R. "Principal-Investigator Status Approved for Medical Center Line Faculty Members." *Stanford Report,* Jan. 29, 2003. http://news-service.stanford.edu/news/2003/january29/mcl.html. Accessed June 2, 2004.

Rossi, P. H. "Researchers, Scholars, and Policy Makers: The Politics of Large-Scale Research." *Daedalus,* 1964, *93,* 1142–1167.

Rubin, E. R., and Lindeman, L. M. *Trends in the Research Enterprise of Academic Health Centers.* Washington, D.C.: Association of Academic Health Centers, 2001.

Schickler, E. *Disjointed Pluralism: Institutional Innovation and the Development of the U.S. Congress.* Princeton, N.J.: Princeton University Press, 2001.

Schuster, J., Smith, D., Corak, K., and Yamada, M. *Strategic Academic Governance: How to Make Big Decisions Better.* Phoenix, Ariz.: Oryx Press, 1994.

Stahler, G. J., and Tash, W. R. "Centers and Institutes in the Research University: Issues, Problems, and Prospects." *Journal of Higher Education,* 1994, *65,* 540–554.

Teich, A. H. "Research Centers and Non-Faculty Researchers: A New Academic Role." In D. I. Powell and B. S. Shen (eds.), *Research in the Age of the Steady-State University.* Boulder, Colo.: Westview Press, 1982.

University of Minnesota. "Governor Announces Historic Partnership Between University of Minnesota and Mayo Clinic." Press release, Apr. 17, 2003.

Yamada, M. "Joint Big Decision Committees and University Governance." In R. Birnbaum (ed.), *Faculty in Governance: The Role of Senates and Joint Committees in Academic Decision Making.* New Directions for Higher Education, no. 75. San Francisco: Jossey-Bass, 1991.

WILLIAM MALLON *is director of organization and management studies at the Association of American Medical Colleges in Washington, D.C.*

6

There is a link between faculty trust of administration and their subsequent levels of participation in the governance process.

A Conceptual Framework of Faculty Trust and Participation in Governance

Myron L. Pope

Trust is a term that is used arbitrarily in daily conversation with little consensus about its true meaning. Moreover, the idea of trust has been explored in the literature as a quality of various facets, including sociology (Coleman, 1990), economics (Fukuyama, 1995), organizational science (Gambetta, 1988; Shaw, 1997), and education (Tshannen-Moran and Hoy, 1998). In this literature, there is an implied notion that trust is paramount to establishing and maintaining positive relationships, whether they are at the interpersonal (Hughes, 1974), group (Barber, 1983), or organizational level (Likert, 1967) in each of these respective fields of study. Research has demonstrated that organizations that develop positive relationships of this nature have benefited from outcomes such as decreased costs and increased risk-taking behavior (Coleman, 1990), as well as increased motivation for collaboration and improved communication (Ghoshal and Bartlett, 1996; Kouzes and Posner, 1993). Trust has also been shown to be even more critical during periods of crisis within an organization (Mayer, Davis, and Schoorman, 1995; Mishra, 1996), when the flexibility of the organization is most tested. The implications of the level of trust in an organization during periods of crisis will often help determine whether an organization will thrive or falter.

Most of the literature that focuses on the influence of trust on organizational culture has stemmed from research in the corporate world (Fukuyama, 1995; Kramer and Tyler, 1996). Within the field of higher education, research on trust has been limited to articles on general public trust of faculty work (Fairweather, 1996), student trust of higher education (Ghosh, Whipple, and Bryan, 2001), faculty trust of administrators (Dufty, 1980), and trust built through strategic planning (Opatz and Hutchinson,

NEW DIRECTIONS FOR HIGHER EDUCATION, no. 127, Fall 2004 © Wiley Periodicals, Inc.

1999). Others have mentioned trust in terms of its general importance to the organizational culture that exists in higher education (Carlisle and Miller, 1998; Lahti, 1979; Miller, McCormack, and Pope, 2000), but no research significantly identifies the importance of trust in shared governance in higher education. It is important to determine whether the positive trust dynamics that exist in corporate society can be developed in the area of governance in higher education.

In this chapter I survey definitions of trust from other fields, along with the perceived importance of trust to organizational stability; review research on organizational culture as a potential foundation for studying faculty trust and faculty participation in the governance process; and analyze the impact of trust on the decision-making process. The final section sets forth potential empirical studies for those interested in the topic. In this context, research can be developed to create a better understanding of the implications of faculty-administrator trust as it relates to institutional governance.

The Foundations of Trust Theory

The following sections provide a framework of reference for the current literature on trust theory. These sections focus on three main aspects of organizational trust: definitions of the term, the role of vulnerability in trust, and the dimensions of trust. Most research on organizational trust treats relationships in the corporate sector and in public high schools. Despite the focus of this literature on hierarchical relationships, as opposed to the seemingly lateral relationships that exist between faculty and administrators in higher education, the foundations established by this literature could be instrumental in introducing baseline conversations and empirical research on trust as it applies to governance in higher education.

Definitions of Trust. Due to the complexity of the meaning of the term *trust,* both conceptually and by definition, there is little consensus on what the term truly implies. Broadly defined, trust is considered to be a "willingness to be vulnerable to the actions of another party based on the expectations that that party will perform an action of importance" (Rousseau, Sitkin, Burt, and Camerer, 1998). In this context, trust anticipates a level of risk and consensual dependence from all parties involved. While these parties are typically aware of the risks of such an arrangement, the risks are not significant in the transaction because the parties realize that there is something at stake for all involved and there is something ultimately to be achieved through this relationship. Opatz and Hutchison (1999) note that trust is not a factor in a relationship if the involved parties have nothing to lose or nothing to gain. Thus, trust is an element in a consensual relationship in which there is equal risk and equal benefit as perceived by the parties involved, and there is a belief that the other party will act in a reciprocal manner.

Vulnerability. Inherent in most research, including the definition of trust by Rousseau and others (1998), is the notion of vulnerability, or the transference of control over a situation to another party. In a relationship in which vulnerability does not exist, Moorman, Deshpande, and Zaltman (1993) note that trust is not important and is "inconsequential for the trustor" (p. 82). They also suggest that uncertainty is a significant part of the trust equation. The implication is that if the trustor is able to control the actions of the exchange partner, there is no need for trust. Ultimately, they contend, if there is a belief that the exchange partner is trustworthy and that the trustor is able to become vulnerable and to accept the reality of an uncertain outcome of the relationship, then trust exists.

Further, as one party becomes more vulnerable to another as a result of this increased trust, it has been suggested that the trusting party may "voluntarily" place resources at the disposal of another or may transfer control over resources to another (Coleman, 1990, p. 100). In this case the trustor exhibits a degree of uncertainty but is not inhibited by this lack of control over the exchange partner's potential actions.

Dimensions of Trust. Beyond this general definition of trust, researchers have identified more specific components that contribute to the trust construct. These factors vary according to the type of relationship at issue—that is, individual, group, or organizational—and they change over the duration of the relationship. One of the more commonly accepted definitions in the literature is that of Mishra (1996), who views trust from a multidimensional perspective and includes the components of competence, openness, benevolence, and reliability in the definition. Some researchers suggest that a fifth dimension, honesty, be added to this formulation of trust (Baier, 1986; Cummings and Bromily, 1996; Butler and Cantrell, 1984; Tschannen-Moran and Hoy, 1998). These various dimensions of trust have been used in research to measure an individual's perception of a corresponding party's trustworthiness in their relations.

The four initial components—competence, openness, benevolence (concern), and reliability—have appeared consistently in the various pieces of literature in which trust is defined. McKnight, Cummings, and Chervany (1998) found that these factors were prevalent in seventy-nine articles and books that dealt with trust, despite the overall complexity of the concept. In their paper, as well as in much of the literature, there seems to be some overlap among the meanings of these four dimensions. At the same time, Mishra (1996) emphasizes that these components of trust combine "multiplicatively in determining the overall degree of trust that one party has with respect to a given referent" (p. 269). Consequently, if one or more of the dimensions were perceived individually as lower than the others, then the overall level of trust would be lower. For example, if an administrator is perceived to be technically competent (competence), open in his or her communications with faculty (openness), and concerned about the welfare of faculty (benevolence), but is inconsistent in his or her actions (reliability), the latter quality acts as a detriment to the former three dimensions that are perceived positively. Thus, organizational trust is the sum of the four dimensions taken from the collective members of the organization.

Implications for Higher Education

In past research, no single study has considered these four dimensions together to assess the level of trust between faculty and administrators. A synthesis of these dimensions could be useful in determining the impact of trust on an institution's system of shared governance and on the level of individual faculty participation in the governance process. Examining trust, including its dimensions, provides a productive means of assessing the relationship between these two groups and of measuring the impact these constructs have on shared institutional governance. To evaluate faculty relationships with administrators accurately, one must recognize the role of trust in motivating faculty involvement in the governance process. This dynamic is inherently tied to the theoretical framework of organizational culture. Thus, this framework will be used to explain the relationship that exists between faculty and administrators.

Organizational Culture and Trust

Institutions of higher education are like other types of organizations in that they can experience lower levels of trust due to their organizational culture. In their assessment of corporate culture, Deshpande and Webster (1989) assert that organizational culture is "the pattern of shared values and beliefs that helps individuals understand organizational functioning and that provides norms for behavior in the organization" (p. 4). They specifically note that trust is affected by the organizational culture that exists within an organization. Referring to previous research (Deshpande and Webster, 1989), Deshpande, Farley, and Webster (1992) describe the difficulty of developing trust in organizations that are more impersonal in nature.

As with other types of organizations, institutions of higher education are highly complex, with many occupational roles, divisions, departments, levels of authority, and operating sites (Price and Mueller, 1986). Moorman, Deshpande, and Zaltman (1993) indicate that this complexity exists even more in terms of variations at the horizontal level in divisions and departments, at the vertical level in terms of levels of authority, and finally in terms of the sites of the organization. This diversity yields situations in which the interpersonal relationships that are important for developing and maintaining trust between individuals are made impossible because of a lack of physical interaction. In addition, the governance of an organization is further complicated by the varying beliefs and norms that exist at these multiple levels.

Dufty (1980) provides an excellent example of these complications in his study. He notes that distance in hierarchical relationships adversely affects trust of academic leadership. Specifically, his research finds that academic staff members are less likely to know what is happening within an organization and are less likely to be able to evaluate occurrences if the physical distance between them and the academic leadership is great. Consequently, in a cross-tabulation of these perceptions with the group's perception of trust, the respondents' level of trust decreased as the level of administration moved higher in the organizational chain. The implications of these findings were that as the decision-making process became more complex and the various levels of administration became more prevalent, the ability to establish trusting, personal relationships became more difficult. Therefore, if physical interaction with constituents at various levels is impossible, to enhance trust within these organizations leaders should strive to maintain opportunities for constituent "buy-in," including inclusion of various levels of constituents in the decision-making process when possible.

Tierney (1988) specifically asserts that it is important for administrators to realize the complexity of the varying cultures that exist within higher education. He suggests that by "understanding organizational culture" individuals can "minimize the occurrence and consequences of cultural conflict and help foster the development of shared goals" (p. 5). Despite the different dynamics that occur at the departmental, institutional, and system levels of higher education, administrators who have a strong understanding of the organizational culture can enhance the performance of their organization by identifying and addressing problems more effectively and efficiently. In this assessment, Tierney provides an organizational framework that includes such constructs as environment, mission, socialization, information, strategy, and leadership. Within this framework, there are a series of questions that administrators must pose to determine their institution's organizational culture. Even though trust is not explicitly mentioned, it is cited indirectly through references to the four dimensions of trust outlined earlier—openness, competence, reliability, and benevolence.

Trust and Governance of Higher Education

Administrators working in institutions of higher education must make themselves aware of the research on organizational culture, specifically as it relates to trust. This research demonstrates that as institutions become more complex, the flow of information and inclusiveness among parties in the decision-making process may be perceived as less than positive. Although it would be impossible for leaders in higher education to involve all constituents in all decisions, they can strive to understand their organizational culture better and to develop shared governance systems, both of which will promote trust within the organization. The final section of this chapter discusses a specific model of governance that is determined by faculty-administrator relationships, a proposed fourth perspective to this model, and suggestions for future research.

A Governance Model Based on Trust. Dufty (1980) indicates that desire for participation in governance varies according to the level of trust present within an organization. He notes that trust depends on the outcomes of the system in question; individuals within a system determine whether to exercise influence in decision making based on whether the outcomes are favorable to them. He explores three levels of participation that are influenced by faculty trust. Political inactivity implies that if individuals within an organization perceive a need to exert influence and have the power to do so, the leadership of the organization is more willing to promote cooperation and inclusion in the decision-making process. In this situation, a more trusting environment can prevail because the leadership recognizes the constituents' potential power and influence in determining decisions. Some, however, might perceive this to be an environment that is not conducive to shared governance. Dufty concludes, to the contrary, that in these environments members of an organization are more accepting of organizational outcomes, even when they may be opposed to them, because they believe they had a true opportunity to participate in the decision-making process. In other words, organizational members may waive their participation in the governance process because they trust the leadership. This level of participation is identified as "political inactivity" (Dufty, 1980, p. 111).

Conversely, Dufty notes that such an unwillingness to participate in the decision-making process may not be a symptom of trust but of "political alienation," a situation in which participants do not have the ability to influence the decision-making process (p. 111). If political alienation occurs, the perceived level of trust is lower in this process. Yet, despite this lower level of trust, which might ordinarily motivate constituents to participate in decision making, certain players are prevented from exerting influence by the bureaucratic nature of the decision-making process.

Finally, Dufty proposes that if there is a low level of trust and organizational players perceive a need and potential ability to influence decision making, they will utilize all resources available to exercise their opportunity to do so. In his definition of this organizational state, Dahl (1961) notes that participants in an organization will utilize "all the resources—opportunities, acts, objects, and so forth—that he can exploit in order to affect the behavior of another" (p. 203). As opposed to a state of political inactivity, in this case the leadership of the organization does not respect the potential influence of the organizational players. Thus, all parties involved are willing to utilize their resources to gain control of the organization's decision-making process. This model has been identified as "political opportunity" (Dufty, 1980, p. 111).

These examples of levels of participation have strong implications for governance of higher education. Individuals will perceive varying levels of trust according to the level of inclusiveness they experience in the governance process. If individuals or groups feel disenfranchised, they may draw on their influence to make changes within the organization. If they are powerless in terms of influence, they must accept the decisions made by the leadership of the organization. However, while they may not have direct influence in the process, these "powerless" individuals may exert power indirectly through the outcomes of employee satisfaction, turnover, and sabotage. These outcomes may seem extreme for higher education, but they are indicative, to a degree, of the behaviors exhibited by faculty members who feel that they have not been included in the governance process. However, these factors have not previously been studied in this context to determine their influence on these outcomes or on other areas, such as institutional effectiveness.

A Fourth Perspective on Governance. A perspective that is not articulated in Dufty's assessment of the impact of trust on faculty participation in governance is one that reflects both a high level of trust and a high level of involvement. In this setting, faculty may insist on being involved in the governance process despite their high levels of trust of the administration. This model is more difficult to explain because it transcends the notion that the relationship between faculty and administrators is adversarial or that the system of governance is one of checks and balances. This model, which I call "political equilibrium," proposes that faculty want to be involved simply for the sake of involvement. The rationale for this particular aspect of involvement needs to be further explored in terms of faculty perceptions of trust in administrators and their reasons for getting involved in the governance process. Inherent in all four models, as well as in the trust literature overall, is the notion that an organization's culture affects the direction and actions of those within the organization (Desphande and Webster, 1989; Tierney, 1988). Understanding organizational culture and its relationship to trust can provide the foundation for future research on faculty-administrator trust.

There is an inherent connection between trust and organizational culture as defined in previous literature. If trust is lacking, others within the organization may be inclined to be more cognizant of, or may even attempt to control the actions of those considered less trustworthy in the organization. This organizational behavior also exists in higher education. However, there is little research to document the actual state of faculty trust of administrators in higher education, or of trust in general in higher education. This chapter provides a conceptual analysis of faculty trust and governance, but empirical data need to be collected to establish more specific frameworks related to the topic.

Future Analyses of Higher Education Trust and Governance

The concept of trust has been defined in the literature primarily with the constructs of openness, competence, reliability, and benevolence at its foundation. These constructs have been empirically tested and have been utilized consistently to measure trust. Thus, assessment measures of administrator trust as perceived by faculty in higher education should be developed based on these studies. In addition, qualitative assessments through faculty interviews can further enhance these studies to determine whether these adapted measures are valid in relationships in higher education. As with the original studies, which used Likert scales, a summation of each of the responses on the instrument will yield an administrator trust score.

To further assess the levels of trust afforded administrators within an institution, the scale can be subdivided to reflect the institution's various administrative levels. This hierarchical evaluation will include opportunities for faculty to measure their trust of departmental (chairs), college (deans), campuswide academic (academic vice president or provost), and institutional (presidential) leadership. The delineation of assessment will provide an opportunity to determine whether Dufty (1980) is correct in concluding that as the closeness of the relationship decreases, so does the level of trust.

Understanding trust and its dimensions is important as an initial step, but the next phase in assessing faculty governance and trust should focus on determining the potential influence of trust on the faculty's desire to be involved in the governance process. Several measures could be used to determine the level of faculty participation in the governance process, including some from Tierney and Minor's 2003 study of faculty governance. The questions in their study focus on the faculty respondents' roles within the governance process, the perceptions of these individuals about the importance and existence of shared governance on their campuses, and the venues in which the faculty participate. Additional questions could be added to determine faculty perceptions of trust within institutional shared governance. Those questions would focus on the importance of trust in shared governance at the respondents' institutions, including the degree to which trust of administrators fluctuates among faculty and the ways in which it influences faculty participation in various levels of governance on their campuses. These questions would be instrumental in providing a yield of the level of faculty participation in the governance process. These measurements of trust and its constructs could also be used to determine whether trust predicts faculty participation in the governance process.

While these questions provide an initial basis for determining faculty levels of participation, there may be other, more effective questions for gaining this information, including analyses of levels of participation based on Dufty's research (1980), along with the fourth model proposed in this chapter.

As institutions differ according to mission, size, governance structure, and other characteristics, it is necessary to analyze various types of institutions to determine the ways in which faculty trust and participation in governance differ within these varying settings. Faculty at these various institutions may have contrasting perceptions of what trust is and how it operates within the governance process. By understanding these differences, a more complete taxonomy of faculty trust in higher education governance can be achieved.

Conclusion

Higher education is being confronted with internal and external dynamics that have complicated the efforts of those within institutions to maintain shared governance. Greater levels of accountability, decreased funding, the increased cost of higher education, the increasing decentralization and departmentalization of academic areas, as well as other factors have made it increasingly impossible to maintain an effective system of shared decision making in higher education. Also, the increased desire for responsive decision making, especially during critical times, sometimes makes the goal of including faculty through traditional methods of participation unattainable. Despite these concerns, shared institutional governance in which faculty have an opportunity to participate in the strategic planning and day-to-day operations of the institution remains an important endeavor. This is particularly true if a positive, productive organizational culture is to be achieved.

As a construct, trust is an adequate indicator of the status of organizational culture. Although it has been analyzed in other fields, the importance of trust has been mentioned sparingly in literature concerning higher education, and it has not yet been examined in terms of its role within the organizational culture of higher education. Many studies of organizational culture in higher education refer to these variables of trust, but no one has looked at these variables collectively. Drawing upon the definition of trust—including its four dimensions of competence, openness, benevolence, and reliability—as established in the tangential literature, faculty and administrators in higher education may use this construct to improve the effectiveness of shared institutional governance.

References

Baier, A. "Trust and Antitrust." *Ethics*, 1986, *96*, 231–260.

Barber, B. *The Logic and Limits of Trust.* New Brunswick, N.J.: Rutgers University Press, 1983.

Butler, J. K., and Cantrell, R. S. "A Behavioral Decision Theory Approach to Modeling Dyadic Trust in Superiors and Subordinates." *Psychological Reports*, 1984, *17*, 643–663.

Carlisle, B. A., and Miller, M. T. *Current Trends and Issues in the Practice of Faculty Involvement in Governance.* 1998. (ED 423 758)

Coleman, J. S. *Foundations of Social Theory.* Cambridge, Mass.: Belknap Press, 1990.

Cummings, L. L., and Bromily, P. "The Organizational Trust Inventory (OTI): Development and Validation." In R. Kramer and T. Tyler (eds.), *Trust in Organizations.* Thousand Oaks, Calif.: Sage, 1996.

Dahl, R. *Who Governs?* New Haven, Conn.: Yale University Press, 1961.

Deshpande, R., Farley, J. U., and Webster, F. E. "Corporate Culture, Customer Orientation, and Innovativeness in Japanese Firms: A Quadrad Analysis." Working paper 92–100. Cambridge, Mass.: Marketing Science Institute, 1992.

Deshpande, R., and Webster, F. E. "Organizational Culture and Marketing: Defining the Research Agenda." *Journal of Marketing*, 1989, *53*, 3–15.

Dufty, N. F. "Trust in Academic Leaders and Committee Operation." *Journal of Tertiary Educational Administration*, 1980, 2(2), 109–122.

Fairweather, J. S. *Faculty Work and Public Trust: Restoring the Value of Teaching and Public Service in American Academic Life*. Needham Heights, Mass.: Allyn & Bacon, 1996.

Fukuyama, F. *Trust: The Social Virtues and the Creation of Prosperity*. New York: Simon & Schuster, 1995.

Gambetta, D. *Trust: Making and Breaking Cooperative Relations*. Cambridge, Mass.: Basil Blackwell, 1988.

Ghosh, A. K., Whipple, T. W., and Bryan, G. A. "Student Trust and Its Antecedents in Higher Education." *Journal of Higher Education*, 2001, 72(3), 322–340.

Ghoshal, S., and Bartlett, C. "Rebuilding Behavioral Context: A Blueprint for Corporate Renewal." *Sloan Management Review*, 1996, 37(2), 23–27.

Hughes, L. W. "Achieving Effective Human Relations and Morale." In J. A. Culbertson, C. Henson, and R. Morrison (eds.), *Performance Objectives for Principals: Concepts and Instruments*. Berkeley, Calif.: McCutchan, 1974.

Kouzes, J. M., and Posner, B. Z. *Credibility*. San Francisco: Jossey-Bass, 1993.

Kramer, R. M., and Tyler, T. (eds.). *Trust in Organizations*. Thousand Oaks, Calif.: Sage, 1996.

Lahti, R. E. *Management and Governance in the Two-Year College*. 1979. (ED 169 984)

Likert, R. *The Human Organization*. New York: McGraw-Hill, 1967.

Mayer, R. C., Davis, J. H., and Schoorman, F. D. "An Integrative Model of Organizational Trust." *Academy of Management Review*, 1995, 20, 709–734.

McKnight, D. H., Cummings, L. L., and Chervany, N. L. "Initial Trust Formation in New Organizational Relationships." *Academy of Management Review*, 1998, 23(3), 473–490.

Miller, M. T., McCormack, T. F., and Pope, M. L. *Sharing Authority in Higher Education: Faculty Involvement in Governance*. 2000. (ED 447 764)

Mishra, A. K. "Organizational Responses to Crisis: The Centrality of Trust." In R. Kramer and T. Tyler (eds.), *Trust in Organizations*. Thousand Oaks, Calif.: Sage, 1996.

Moorman, C., Deshpande, R., and Zaltman, G. "Factors Affecting Trust in Market Research Relationships." *Journal of Marketing*, 1993, 57, 81–101.

Opatz, P., and Hutchinson, K. "Building Trust Through Strategic Planning." *Planning for Higher Education*, 1999, 27, 21–27.

Price, J. L., and Mueller, C. W. *Handbook of Organizational Measurement*. London: Pitman Press, 1986.

Rousseau, D., Sitkin, S. B., Burt, R., and Camerer, C. "Not So Different After All: A Cross-Discipline View of Trust." *Academy of Management Review*, 1998, 23(3), 393–404.

Shaw, R. B. *Trust in the Balance: Building Successful Organizations on Results, Integrity, and Concerns*. San Francisco: Jossey-Bass, 1997.

Tierney, W. G. "Organizational Culture in Higher Education." *Journal of Higher Education*, 1988, 59(1), 2–21.

Tierney, W. G., and Minor, J. T. *Challenges for Governance: A National Report*. Los Angeles: Center for Higher Education Policy Analysis, University of Southern California, 2003.

Tschannen-Moran, M., and Hoy, W. K. "A Conceptual and Empirical Analysis of Trust in Schools." *Journal of Educational Administration*, 1998, 36, 334–352.

MYRON L. POPE *is the assistant vice president of student services at the University of Central Oklahoma.*

7

Cultural and symbolic processes—that is, communication—quite frequently play as important a role as structural issues in enabling effective governance.

A Cultural Perspective on Communication and Governance

William G. Tierney, James T. Minor

"I find it ironic," said one professor, "that you can be a faculty member here and never hear from the senate. You would think there would be some correspondence, or the representative from your school would come to faculty meetings to provide some indication of what the senate is doing." The professor's observation is on target. The role of communication in the governance of academic organizations is frequently underestimated or, more likely, ignored. Instead, studies of governance generally involve structural or role-related analysis. Some scholars discuss the strengths and weaknesses of an academic senate or assembly, for example, and consider its size, composition, and functions in relation to its effectiveness. Others evaluate the relative power of a particular position within a governing body, such as the presidency, or the role of mid-level functionaries, such as department chairs or deans.

In this chapter we consider the role of communication in academic governance. We suggest that to become more effective in governance, faculty should focus on communicative strategies in addition to structural reforms. All too often, however, when faculty believe that their power is diminished or that their voice is limited, they argue solely for structural changes to one or another academic body. Although we do not dispute that on some campuses an overhaul of a decision-making body such as an academic senate is useful, we assert that it is necessary to consider the interpretive potential of organizational life. Colleges and universities are not simply the sum of the structural units that produce and disseminate knowledge within them; they are also places where symbolic and abstract cultural

NEW DIRECTIONS FOR HIGHER EDUCATION, no. 127, Fall 2004 © Wiley Periodicals, Inc.   85 meanings are created. From an interpretive perspective, these symbols and meanings are in part the byproduct of the cultural processes that an organization's actors create in communicating with one another. It is these processes and communicative acts that we wish to consider here. We argue that the culture of the organization determines communication, and that communication helps constitute governance.

Our two reference points for analysis are a survey of shared governance that included 763 institutions and a group of eight case studies of four-year colleges and universities. We begin with an overview of the communicative frameworks of governance and then discuss three central aspects of communication: situated meaning, speech and literacy events, and symbols and ceremonies. The goals of the chapter are to highlight the ways in which people communicate with one another and to suggest that communication is a key component of successful shared governance.

Governance by Conversation

Lewis B. Mayhew (1974) wrote the following about the governance structure of the modern university: "In one sense the governance of [the] university is governance by conversation. Many of the seemingly critical matters, such as the form of the curriculum or even the size of the budget . . . are the subject of thousands of hours of consultation and conversation before a final decision is ratified" (p. 58). Indeed, it would be impossible to chart how decisions are made in a traditional college or university. Unlike in a business, where an organizational map can at least approximate the path of decision making, at a college or university ideas rarely follow a specific route to their implementation. When one looks, for example, at the issues before faculty senates at different colleges and universities, one finds that issues vary among institutions and even within institutions from one year to the next. Further, at some institutions senates are key faculty-governing bodies, while at other locales they are inconsequential or non-existent (Tierney and Minor, 2003). In a universe of four thousand postsecondary institutions, one certainly can expect a degree of variability among senates. In some senates, for example, all faculty are included, while in others faculty are represented by academic unit or popular vote. In some cases executive committees are chosen by the entire faculty, in others they are selected by the senate itself. Some senate presidents are elected faculty members, while others are the president or academic vice president of the institution.

Structurally, then, one cannot anticipate that a specific governing body will deal with particular issues regardless of institutional type or context. Among institutions, however, the delineation of formal faculty voice is relatively clear. More than 75 percent of the respondents to the survey stated that faculty had substantial influence in determining undergraduate curriculum, standards for promotion and tenure, and standards for the evaluation of teaching. There was equal agreement among participants that faculty had relatively little formal influence in setting budget priorities or evaluating the president and provost. Perceptual indicators, however, show divergent views. For example, when asked about the quality of communication among campus constituents in decision making, 88 percent of academic vice presidents agreed that it was good, or sufficient to make progress, compared to just 66 percent of faculty who agreed.

Although faculty claimed to have little formal influence in certain types of decisions, they reported having considerable informal influence. Both formal and informal influence were evident in many different types of governance structures. Although more than 85 percent of all four-year institutions have some form of a faculty-governing body, most individuals reported academic departments, standing faculty committees, and ad-hoc committees as substantial venues for participation. One faculty member of twenty-six years responded: "Like many other institutions, we make decisions based on the outcomes of multiple formal and informal conversations."

One commonsense observation of this process is that, among organizations, structures vary a great deal. Regardless of which venues are employed for deliberations by faculty, decisions are reached through communicative processes that take place within and outside those structures. Our point here is more than simply to assert that one group communicates by formal pathways and another by informal means. We suggest that the manner in which groups communicate with one another highlights underlying cultural beliefs within the organization. In turn, the way in which a college or university's actors create the culture of the organization determines a host of critical issues pertaining to the faculty's role in governance.

Accordingly, if it is determined that faculty voice should be increased or taken more seriously in the governance of an institution, then an appropriate strategy for achieving this goal would be to consider the communicative processes employed within the organization. One fruitful way to analyze organizational communication is to consider how meaning is situated, what constitutes speech and literacy events, and how communicative symbols and ceremonies are used and by whom. As will become clear, each of these ideas frames an understanding of how communication functions as a cultural process within an organization.

Situated Meaning. Linguists have defined *situated meaning* as an understanding of the specific context that is transformed and negotiated by rules of speaking, which reflect the actors' relationships to, and attitudes toward, one another and the issues under consideration (Hymes, 1974). Although rules exist in any institution, in an academic organization populated by highly verbal participants who frequently seek to understand underlying structures, they are particularly important. Thus, we need to come to terms not only with the contexts in which communication takes place, such as a faculty senate, and the actors involved in the specific structure, such as a senate president, but also with the wider sociopolitical structures in which the communicative processes are embedded.

Investigations of shared governance need to move away from purely structural or outcome-related analysis. Looking only to a senate, for example, to define the types of issues that will be addressed ignores the ways in which messages are created by the organization's culture. Similarly, to argue simply that the faculty's power and authority can be gauged by decisions made in a senate or committee is to disregard the idea that communication transcends decisions and outcomes. No one has ever plausibly advanced the argument that any one system of shared governance is better than the rest, nor has anyone demonstrated that a particular system necessitates that faculty bodies formally vote on all issues that come before it.

To consider the situated meaning of communication, one must identify who is and who is not involved in governance, the venues where governance takes place, and the formal and informal means used to communicate. Such an approach has broad implications for the study and analysis of shared governance. Studies of academic decision making frequently describe faculty governance in either-or terms: either an institution has an effective faculty senate or its system of faculty governance is a sham. Rather than assume that everyone must participate in faculty governance for it to be effective, we posit that the history, culture, and present contexts of an institution frame governance in important ways. What Clark (1970) defined as a "distinctive college" (p. 234), for example, might have active faculty involvement on myriad topics, whereas a research university might seek faculty engagement in only a handful of issues. A campus with collective bargaining is likely to communicate in ways quite different from a campus without such an agreement. The point of our analysis is not to determine the best structure of governance for all institutions, or to imply that certain roles must have more authority. Instead, we seek to explore how an organization's participants make meaning based on the confines of the institutional context.

Literacy and Speech Events. A literacy event takes place when a piece of writing plays an integral role in shaping meaning and interactions among participants. Speech events are oral in nature and surround literacy events. As Heath (1982) has noted, "Speech events may describe, repeat, reinforce, expand, frame or contradict written materials, and participants must learn whether the oral or written mode takes precedence in literacy events" (p. 93). Obviously, in an academic community a wealth of literacy events takes place, and speech events circumscribe organizational decisions. With the advent of Web sites and the Internet, literacy events have increased dramatically, just as conference calls and voice-activated referencing have led to an increase in speech events. A student newspaper, a faculty forum, a university newspaper, a senate Web page, and the minutes and agenda for meetings are examples of literacy events. Each piece of writing pertains to some aspect of decision making. It informs various constituencies about either decisions to be made or actions taken. Writing may be used to explain actions, to argue for or against a particular idea, or to inform debate. Written materials help shape an argument.

Speech events generally take place with participants face-to-face and involve literacy events. Individuals may refer to a text or extrapolate from it, confer individually or as a group, and so on. They might speak formally or informally. An example of a formal speech act that involves a literacy event would be the approval of meeting minutes with changes to the written text suggested orally by a committee member. An example of an informal speech event that involves literacy events could be the gossip or conversation that occurs before or after a meeting about a memo that has been sent or received.

Speech and literacy events, then, are oral and written messages communicated to an organization's constituencies. Such messages have distinct temporal frames. They can be divided into four types: preparational, presentational, preservational, and promotional. Each event has not only a distinct time frame but also a purpose within that time frame. For example, before making necessary changes to the institution, a group may utilize a Web page to develop white papers that discuss why the faculty need to revamp general education. Or, perhaps, when a presentation is being prepared for a curricular affairs committee, ideas for specific changes may be debated among faculty. Once decisions of any type are made, a faculty handbook may be amended to create institutional memory of the revision. Finally, one may utilize a literacy event to promote and communicate decisions that have been made by the governing body. Such analysis enables us to understand how members make use of particular documents and materials within governance.

When analyzing literacy and speech events, the roles of central and peripheral actors need to be considered. This information is particularly important with regard to shared governance because speech events occur between speakers and listeners. Similarly, a literacy event is an interaction over a text that someone has written and someone reads. Consider, for example, perhaps the most serious action an academic community might contemplate: the removal of an individual faculty member's tenure. Numerous literacy events come into play—the faculty handbook, the institution's grievance policy, and all documents pertaining directly to the case. The dismissal proceedings and the hearings of the case are examples of speech events. In analyzing these speech events, it is necessary to consider carefully who instigates the proceedings and who is involved in the hearings. These events are not disembodied scripts devoid of speakers, listeners, authors, and readers. If a faculty committee brings forth a cause for dismissal, the meaning of the scripts may well differ from those if the administration were to do the same. Literacy and speech events inevitably are defined by the situated meaning infused by an organization's actors, history, and culture.

In one light, the kind of analysis described here does little more than state the obvious: minutes are taken at senate meetings, and individuals make oral changes to written documents that are then preserved. A university president's memo to the faculty about general education carries different meanings than an assistant professor's message on a faculty listserv. In this chapter, however, we argue a different point. Shared governance is more than a functional analysis of whether faculty members vote on a particular issue or whether a certain clause exists in the faculty handbook to guarantee protections. Shared governance is a cultural undertaking that reinscribes what the academic community believes about itself. These beliefs help define the speakers, listeners, authors, and readers of speech and literacy events. Just as one needs to analyze the specific protections guaranteed to faculty in a contract to ensure that academic freedom is preserved, a college or university must attend to the cultural interpretations given to communication to achieve effective governance. To ignore these interpretations permits an incomplete understanding of academic governance.

Communicative Symbols and Ceremonies. Manifest messages of governance and the latent and symbolic cultural meanings of an institution also merit attention. As Feldman and March observed, "Organizational structures and processes often have symbolic importance to participants" (Birnbaum, 1989, p. 428). The composition of faculty senates and university committees, the absence or presence of the president at a meeting, and the participation or absence of the provost in promotion and tenure meetings all send messages to the community about governance. These messages are highly unstable and vary from campus to campus. They change over time and exemplify the latent and shifting cultural meanings created within academic communities.

Active faculty participation in governance might indicate to the academic world that a college or university is in the postsecondary mainstream. A for-profit college that relies entirely on part-time faculty who utilize distance learning may seek to legitimize itself by creating a virtual academic senate to prove that it is not so different from traditional institutions. The addition of a promotion and tenure committee that includes requirements about the need to do research at an institution that has no history of doing research may signify that the university aims to rise in the traditional academic hierarchy. Statements about academic freedom that refer to the American Association of University Professors (1966) place an institution in line with mainstream ideas about the topic. Conversely, a statement that stipulates a narrow interpretation of academic freedom made by a representative of a religious institution may be a purposeful symbolic message that the college or university has made a conscious decision to distance itself from the mainstream.

It is important to recognize that symbols and ceremonies, as interpretive acts, rarely have a singular meaning. A president's absence from senate meetings may indicate that the president's schedule is too full, but senators may interpret this absence as an affront to shared governance. The faculty's extended deliberations over a move to dismiss a colleague accused of terrorist acts may appear to external constituencies as foot-dragging, whereas the faculty may perceive it to be evidence of their devotion to due process and academic freedom. A faculty committee that votes to move from an all-faculty assembly to a smaller group of elected representatives may be motivated by trying to increase faculty voice. However, others might see the change as an attempt to stifle faculty voice. Attending to the symbolic side of academic life is necessary to improve governance. Therefore, those who seek to rethink how governance functions at their institution need to take into account the specific symbolic and cultural meanings that infuse an organization's structures.

Perceptions of governance on a campus are determined in part by the ceremonies and culture that exist within those organizational structures. Ceremonies are important sites for the analysis of the values of an academic community. At some institutions, for example, during convocation, a faculty member, perhaps the president of the senate, will lead the procession of faculty, administrators, and graduates in the ceremony. The message of this action is that the faculty "lead" the institution. Similarly, when faculty recommend candidates for an honorary doctorate to a board of trustees, they simultaneously highlight their ceremonial and "real" roles in shared governance. Ceremonies provide individuals with a sense of membership and integration in an organization. They convey to faculty that they are not simply members of a guild, rather that they play a central role in determining the institution's well-being and future. An organization deprived of ceremonies that celebrate or dramatize organizational values is one in which little explicit attention is paid to the cultural aspects of academic life. A de-ritualized organization is one bereft of meaning. In such cases, the actors have assumed that the institution is a collection of instrumentalities in which decisions are made through chains of command. While one cannot dispute the benefits of effective and efficient procedures for an institution, if one ignores the cultural aspects of organizational life, one runs the risk of overlooking the invisible bonds of communal affiliation that tie the professorate to their institution and to one another.

Improving Communication and Governance

For those who subscribe to a cultural view of the academic world and are concerned about enhancing faculty involvement in governance, there are at least two central suggestions that logically follow the arguments raised here.

Focus on Communicative Pathways. David Leslie has argued cogently (1996) that "change in colleges and universities comes when it happens in the trenches; what faculty and students do is what the institution becomes. It does not happen because a committee or a president asserts a new idea" (p. 110). Unfortunately, there is often a temptation to revert to old-fashioned notions of power, so "where the buck stops" indicates who has the final authority. If the buck does not pass by the faculty or if individuals believe that the buck actually stops at the faculty's doorstep, then governance does not appear to be shared. From a cultural perspective, however, governance needs to be more than a basic check of who gets to vote and who is denied the opportunity to do so.

Shared governance does not result solely from the formal allocation of spheres of responsibility and authority (Trow, 1990). Instead, informal arrangements and processes should be interpreted by the academic collective with regard to the relative influence of different academic bodies and the significance of different decisions. It is important to recognize that faculty involvement in governance occurs on many levels and in many forums. Simply because faculty do not vote on a preponderance of issues does not mean that shared governance is not functioning. Meaningful involvement is achieved when multiple constituencies are able to communicate with one another across multiple venues.

Colleges and universities exist in "loosely coupled" environments (Weick, 1976, p. 3). A mistaken tendency among those attempting to improve faculty governance is to try to tighten this loose coupling. Far too often individuals assume that for meaningful engagement to occur all decisions must be processed through a governance structure such as a senate. Such a mindset creates the potential for faculty governance to deal with just a few issues over the course of a year. Instead, those involved would be better advised to accept that institutions exist in decentralized organizations and that the faculty's engagement with an issue may be sporadic. Effective governance, then, is defined not so much by the presence of an efficient structure or by the number of votes the faculty concludes in a year. Effective governance pertains more to the understanding and management of meaning such that the core values of the faculty and of the institution are not merely preserved, but advanced.

Accept the Potency of Speech and Literacy Events. Those who understand the symbolic functions of speech and literacy events within an organization are more likely to use these communicative vehicles than those who ignore them. At a time when faculty have numerous communicative outlets at their disposal, it is imperative that they use them in a systematic fashion. As analysis of typical speech and literacy events at colleges or universities demonstrates, too often it appears as if the administration owns the airwaves. The alumni office puts out the university magazine. The president's office issues quarterly newsletters. The provost's office publishes a weekly news magazine and has periodic e-updates to advertise a particular idea. The provost currently is engaged in writing a strategic plan and has sent drafts to the entire faculty asking for feedback. The office of information services reports to the vice president for administration and manages the university's Web site. The deans send out weekly bulletins on listservs for their individual schools and send out a biannual update to donors, alumni, students, and faculty regarding the state of the school.

Meanwhile, the faculty senate tries to publish one or two newsletters a year that arrive three months late. Their Web site seldom is updated, so one is never really sure what topics are being addressed. The faculty have created a campuswide listserv, but after a heated debate about whether faculty messages should be edited or simply published, only two kinds of messages have appeared: occasional announcements about sublets from faculty who are about to depart on sabbatical, and messages from three professors who do not hesitate to use the listserv to expound on their most recent complaint. As a result, a third of the faculty also has removed itself from the listserv.

Such a portrait may seem like a caricature of academic life, but unfortunately, this scenario often closely reflects the reality of the situation. Some will respond that the administration naturally does a better job of communicating with the academic community, as they have both resources and time at their disposal. At the same time, some leaders are better at symbolic management than others. Faculty who are concerned about governance need to consider ways to communicate a message in a timely, concerted, and systematic manner. Yet, in an era when technology has increased our capability to communicate, faculty communication with one another and with university administration seems to have only decreased. Administrators have mastered ways to get their message out. In contrast, faculty often do not seem to recognize the importance of communication, which returns us to the central precept of this chapter.

Communication is not a cure-all for the current woes that confront those involved in shared governance, but a concern for organizational reform must be balanced with an awareness of the communicative codes within the workplace. Academic organizations are rich in cultural meanings. Intellectual work, in part, involves the understanding, decoding, and manipulation of symbolic messages. If faculty follow such methods in their intellectual endeavors, they can use a similar, critical approach in their efforts to improve shared governance within their academic communities.

References

American Association of University Professors. "Statement on Government of Colleges and Universities." Washington, D.C.: American Association of University Professors, 1966. [http://www.aaup.org/statements/Redbook/Govern.htm].

Clark, B. *The Distinctive College: Antioch, Reed, and Swarthmore.* Chicago: Aldine, 1970.

Heath, S. "Protean Shapes in Literacy Events." In D. Tanned (ed.), *Spoken and Written Language.* Norwood, N.J.: Ablex, 1982.

Hymes, D. "Ways of Speaking." In R. Bauman and J. Sherzer (eds.), *Explorations in the Ethnography of Speaking.* Cambridge: Cambridge University Press, 1974.

Leslie, D. "Strategic Governance: The Wrong Questions?" *Review of Higher Education,* 1996, *20*(1), 101–112.

Mayhew, L. B. "Administration and Governance of the University." Unpublished manuscript, 1974.

Tierney, W. G., and Minor, J. T. "Challenges for Governance: A National Report." Los Angeles: Center for Higher Education Policy Analysis, University of Southern California, 2003.

Trow, M. "The Academic Senate as a School for University Leadership." *Liberal Education*, 1990, 76(1), 23–27.

Weick, K. E. "Educational Organizations as Loosely Coupled Systems." *Administrative Science Quarterly*, 1976, 21(1), 1–19.

WILLIAM G. TIERNEY is *Wilbur-Kieffer Professor of Higher Education and director of the Center for Higher Education Policy Analysis at the Rossier School of Education, University of Southern California.*

JAMES T. MINOR is *an assistant professor of higher education in the HALE Program at Michigan State University.*

8

*A number of significant studies of shared governance have
been carried out in the last decade.*

Exploring Current Issues on Shared Governance

Vicente M. Lechuga

Shared governance is a unique characteristic of the U.S. higher education
system; it is often misunderstood and difficult to define. This confusion
leads to problematic decision-making structures that impair the governance
process. Much of the debate regarding shared governance pertains to the
roles faculty, administrators, and governing boards play in the decision-
making process.

The 1991 issue of *New Directions for Higher Education* (Birnbaum,
1991) was devoted in its entirety to shared governance and was the last *New
Directions* volume dedicated to the topic. His issue, along with this one, can
be taken as two parts of a compendium. What follows is an annotated bibliography that lists seminal works and other important articles that have
been published since 1991. The purpose of this chapter is to provide a
greater understanding of shared governance by focusing on the most recent
and significant literature.

Association of Governing Boards of Universities and Colleges. "Renewing
the Academic Presidency: Stronger Leadership for Tougher Times." Report
of the Commission on the Academic Presidency. Washington, D.C.: Association of Governing Boards of Universities and Colleges, 1996.

In 1996, the Association of Governing Boards of Universities and
Colleges released a report emphasizing the need for stronger, more effective
presidential leadership. The report supports the tenets of shared governance
as a valuable asset of the U.S. higher education system and states the need
for effective leadership at our institutions of higher education in order to

NEW DIRECTIONS FOR HIGHER EDUCATION, no. 127, Fall 2004 © Wiley Periodicals, Inc.

restore public trust in colleges and universities. However, the report cites the need for presidents to make quick decisions with more discretion and less consultation.

Bowen, W. G. *Inside the Boardroom: Governance by Directors and Trustees.* New York: Wiley, 1994.

The author has served on several boards of nonprofit institutions, including Princeton University; in this book he explores the role of the board of directors in for-profit and nonprofit corporations. He offers recommendations on how boards can serve the interests of organizations and their stakeholders better and provides a unique perspective on improving the function of governing boards.

Collins, L. "Shared Governance in the California Community Colleges." *Academe,* 2002, *88*(4), 36–40.

With the passage of Assembly Bill 1725, the practice of shared governance expanded in the California community colleges. The author contends that management fads such as total quality management undermine the practice of collegiality, focusing on corporate management approaches that negate faculty voice and increase the authority of college and university presidents.

Duderstadt, J. J. *A University for the Twenty-First Century.* Ann Arbor: University of Michigan Press, 2000.

The author discusses rapid changes taking place in higher education and the economic, social, and technological forces that drive these changes. He argues that universities that are able to adapt quickly to such changes will lead the way into the twenty-first century, and he advocates for increased presidential authority.

Hamilton, N. "The Academic Profession's Leadership Role in Shared Governance." *Liberal Education,* 2000, *86*(3), 12–19.

The author explores shared governance and leadership concepts in the context of the "four original learned professions"—law, medicine, ministry, and the professoriate. He discusses faculty members' leadership roles and examines their primary responsibilities in shared governance. He posits that the profession's major threat will be from individuals within the professoriate who feel that faculty members' beliefs are subject to public scrutiny.

Leslie, D. W., and Fretwell, E. K. *Wise Moves in Hard Times: Creating and Managing Resilient Colleges and Universities.* San Francisco: Jossey-Bass, 1996.

Changes in the higher education environment, such as decreasing financial resources, call for increased accountability, and public criticisms of colleges and universities pose challenges to institutions of higher education. The authors describe processes that can help strengthen colleges and universities and assert that by modifying mission, organization, teaching, and learning, institutions of higher education can adapt to the changing environment.

Longin, T. C. "Institutional Governance: A Call for Collaborative Decision Making in American Higher Education." In W. G. Berberet and L. A. McMillin (eds.), *A New Academic Compact: Revisioning the Relationship Between Faculty and their Institutions.* Bolton, Mass.: Anker, 2002.

The author argues that in the rapidly changing environment of higher education, current governance structures and processes are deficient. The author highlights themes from an "academic compact" proposed by the Associated New American Colleges and maintains that faculty members play a central role in institutional decision making. He recommends that boards, administrators, and faculty create structures that reward faculty involvement in governance activities.

Phillips, I. V. "Shared Governance on Black College Campuses." *Academe,* 2002, *88*(4), 50–55.

The author discusses several areas in which shared governance is lacking and asserts that boards of trustees at historically black colleges and universities (HBCUs) exercise greater authority over institutions than do their white counterparts. The author contends that many HBCUs are still segregated in the sense that they lack the necessary funding to improve programs and facilities, hence few non-black students choose to attend.

Ramo, K. J. *Assessing the Faculty's Role in Shared Governance: Implications of AAUP Standards.* Washington, D.C.: American Association of University Professors, 1998.

This guide identifies and summarizes references in the *American Association of University Professors Redbook,* a collection of policy documents concerning faculty members' rights and responsibilities, relating to faculty members' roles in governance. Its purpose is to assess the implications of those references for individuals who may have questions regarding faculty roles in shared governance at their particular institution.

Rosovsky, H. "Some Thoughts About University Governance." In W. Hirscht and L. Weber (eds.), *Leadership: Where Else Can We Go?* Durham, N.C.: Duke University Press, 2001.

The author maintains that university governance would be improved by removing "extreme" democracy, and contends that university presidents should be provided with greater authority. He argues that institutional governance should center on the improvement of teaching, learning, and research; this requires the careful use of "scarce factors" such as faculty time.

Scott, J. W. "Death by Inattention: The Strange Fate of Faculty Governance." *Academe,* 1997, *83,* 28–33.

The author posits that faculty have become ineffective decision makers because they have overlooked the decline in faculty participation in governance and take for granted their authority over professional and academic matters.

Reference

Birnbaum, R. (ed.). *Faculty in Governance: The Role of Senates and Joint Committees in Academic Decision Making.* New Directions for Higher Education, no. 75. San Francisco: Jossey-Bass, 1991.

VICENTE M. LECHUGA *is a research assistant in the Center for Higher Education Policy Analysis, University of Southern California, involved in a three-year research project that is analyzing and recommending ways to improve shared governance in four-year colleges and universities.*

INDEX

Back Issue/Subscription Order Form

Copy or detach and send to:

Jossey-Bass, A Wiley Company, 989 Market Street, San Francisco CA 94103-1741

Call or fax toll-free: Phone 888-378-2537 6:30AM – 3PM PST; Fax 888-481-2665

Back Issues: Please send me the following issues at $29 each
(Important: please include series initials and issue number, such as HE114.)

_____

_____

_____

$ _____ Total for single issues

$ _____ SHIPPING CHARGES: SURFACE   Domestic   Canadian

	Domestic	Canadian
First Item	$5.00	$6.00
Each Add'l Item	$3.00	$1.50

For next-day and second-day delivery rates, call the number listed above.

Subscriptions: Please __start __renew my subscription to *New Directions for Higher Education* for the year 2____at the following rate:

U.S.	__Individual $80	__Institutional $170
Canada	__Individual $80	__Institutional $210
All Others	__Individual $104	__Institutional $244
Online Subscription		__Institutional $170
Print and Online Subscription		__Institutional $187

**For more information about online subscriptions visit
www.interscience.wiley.com**

$ _____ Total single issues and subscriptions (Add appropriate sales tax for your state for single issue orders. No sales tax for U.S. subscriptions. Canadian residents, add GST for subscriptions and single issues.)

__Payment enclosed (U.S. check or money order only)

__VISA __MC __AmEx #_____ Exp. Date _____

Signature _____ Day Phone _____

__ Bill Me (U.S. institutional orders only. Purchase order required.)

Purchase order # _____

Federal Tax ID13559302   GST 89102 8052

Name _____

Address _____

_____

Phone _____ E-mail _____

For more information about Jossey-Bass, visit our Web site at www.josseybass.com

NEW DIRECTIONS FOR HIGHER EDUCATION IS NOW AVAILABLE ONLINE AT WILEY INTERSCIENCE

What is Wiley InterScience?

Wiley InterScience is the dynamic online content service from John Wiley & Sons delivering the full text of over 300 leading scientific, technical, medical, and professional journals, plus major reference works, the acclaimed *Current Protocols* laboratory manuals, and even the full text of select Wiley print books online.

What are some special features of Wiley InterScience?

Wiley InterScience Alerts is a service that delivers table of contents via e-mail for any journal available on Wiley InterScience as soon as a new issue is published online.
Early View is Wiley's exclusive service presenting individual articles online as soon as they are ready, even before the release of the compiled print issue. These articles are complete, peer-reviewed, and citable.
CrossRef is the innovative multi-publisher reference linking system enabling readers to move seamlessly from a reference in a journal article to the cited publication, typically located on a different server and published by a different publisher.

How can I access Wiley InterScience?

Visit http://www.interscience.wiley.com

Guest Users can browse Wiley InterScience for unrestricted access to journal Tables of Contents and Article Abstracts, or use the powerful search engine.
Registered Users are provided with a *Personal Home Page* to store and manage customized alerts, searches, and links to favorite journals and articles. Additionally, Registered Users can view free Online Sample Issues and preview selected material from major reference works.
Licensed Customers are entitled to access full-text journal articles in PDF, with select journals also offering full-text HTML.

How do I become an Authorized User?

Authorized Users are individuals authorized by a paying Customer to have access to the journals in Wiley InterScience. For example, a university that subscribes to Wiley journals is considered to be the Customer. Faculty, staff and students authorized by the university to have access to those journals in Wiley InterScience are Authorized Users. Users should contact their Library for information on which Wiley journals they have access to in Wiley InterScience.

ASK YOUR INSTITUTION ABOUT WILEY INTERSCIENCE TODAY!